I0469243

DAVID and GOLIATH in the MODERN COURT

Extraordinary Trial Experiences of a Lawyer in the Philippines

Virgilio J. Santiago

Order this book online at www.trafford.com
or email orders@trafford.com

Most Trafford titles are also available at major online book retailers.

© Copyright 2010 Virgilio J. Santiago.
All rights reserved. No part of this publication may be reproduced, stored in a retrieval
system, or transmitted, in any form or by any means, electronic, mechanical, photocopying,
recording, or otherwise, without the written prior permission of the author.

Printed in the United States of America.

ISBN: 978-1-4269-4571-7 (sc)
ISBN: 978-1-4269-4572-4 (hc)
ISBN: 978-1-4269-4573-1 (e)

Library of Congress Control Number: 2010915293

*Our mission is to efficiently provide the world's finest, most comprehensive book publishing
service, enabling every author to experience success. To find out how to publish your book,
your way, and have it available worldwide, visit us online at www.trafford.com*

Trafford rev. 10/27/2010

 www.trafford.com

North America & international
toll-free: 1 888 232 4444 (USA & Canada)
phone: 250 383 6864 ◆ fax: 812 355 4082

"I humbly acknowledge the presence, aid and assistance of God Almighty and thank Him endlessly for allowing me to win my cases for His greater honor and glory".

Virgilio J. Santiago.
Philippine lawyer

Table of Contents

Prologue

God without man is God;

Man without God is nothing;

Man is born to praise and glorify the Lord God Almighty

The Law Profession is an honorable, respectable and dignified Profession;

Lawyers are likened to the knight in shining armour, ever

devoted to fight evil, to save the oppressed and to crush the oppressor.

Lawyers are compensated not only with treasure, pleasure and honor, but

More, with the right to right a wrong;

Man is not born just "To Work To Eat" nor, "To Eat To Work"

Man is born to fight evil, for has it not been said. that:"For evil to triumph is for good men to do nothing to stop it."

The Law Profession is the vehicle to stop evil.

Virgilio J. Santiago
Philippine Lawyer
2610 Presidente Street,
Stockton, CA 95210 - USA
Tel. (209) 957-0670
e-mail: vjsan51536@yahoo.com

Chapter I
Exordium

I was born in 1936 in Sampaloc district, Manila, Philippines. My mother Aurea Jimenez Santiago was a teacher in a government run public elementary school while my father Guillermo Santiago wrote poems in Pilipino language for books and magazines in Tagalog vernacular sold for general consumption in Manila City while also working as advertising agent for a newspaper daily with general circulation in Manila and throughout the Philippines.

During my youth I had no ambition. All I wanted to do then was to build my own family with my childhood sweetheart and live a simple life, thus I stopped going to school and told my mother that I would just drive the passenger jeepney of our neighbor- lawyer on commission basis, earn money and marry my sweetheart. My mother protested as I expected and almost cried as she said to me: "My son what you wanted to do is a mistake and childish, it is hard to be driving the whole day for commission of a meager sum while running all kinds of risk. If you run over a pedestrian by accident you will be arrested and charged in court, who will bail you out?, How will you pay your lawyer? Lawyers are costly and court hearings run a long way., In the meantime who will feed your wife, your son, your family? My son the wiser thing you should do is to go back to school, finish high school, go to college, be a lawyer.

"The law profession is a noble profession, respectable, dignified profession. A lawyer is likened to a knight in shining armour, ever ready to fight for the oppressed and the weak. A lawyer is compensated not

1

only with treasure, pleasure and honor, but more, with the right to right a wrong.

"Our country is a developing poor country. People get arrested without warrant of arrest by abusive police. The ignorant do not resist because they do not know their rights, while the poor cannot resist because they have no money to pay lawyers who charge excessive fees. Have you not heard of farmers who had been in possession of the land, tilled the land, planted the land and took care of the land since their fathers' grandfathers', grandfathers' fathers' time but who were suddenly driven away from their land for trespassing by some rich people who had managed to gain title to the land overnight with the aid of unscrupulous, corrupt government officials who had exchanged the honor and sanctity of their office with the gold, guns and goons of the rich. See? There were people in prison not because they were guilty of the crime with which they were charged but because of their misfortune to be born poor and cannot pay their lawyers to fight their cases. While there were lawyers called public defenders whose salaries were paid by the government out of peoples' taxes their salaries were not commensurate with the too many cases of the poor they had to handle so that just to finish some of their cases they usually advice the accused to admit guilt to a lesser offense or to admit guilt for a lower term of imprisonment; sometimes they were seen fighting the case to termination but their effort isseen to bebelow par in terms of preparation and determination as compared to the highly paid lawyers in private practice thus the number of disgruntled citizens in the hills grew in time. Some became kidnappers, some highway robbers, while some terrorists, shaking the government and made the country unsafe, and drove away tourists who were rich source of revenue for our country; have you not heard of politicians who ran for public office on pretentious desire to serve the people but once elected became the master of the people and the people their servants. My son gone was the time when public officials were honest and honorable and were incorruptible. They value their honor more than life.

"Evil has crept into public service.

"Remember my son, people are born in this world not just "to work to eat" nor just "to eat to work" but to fight evil and to do justice to 'honor and glorify' the Good Lord God Almighty. I will pray for you son."

Nonetheless, I totally disregarded my mother's admonition and advice.

I became a driver of the passenger jeepney of our neighbor-lawyer.

Chapter II
The 'U" Turn

(Names*fictional/events factual)

One day while I was driving along the usual route for passenger jeepneys at the Ramon Magsaysay Boulevard (named in honor of President Ramon Magsaysay of the Philippines) in front of the University of the East Ramon Magsaysay Memorial Hospital, a motorcycle recklessly bumped and struck the rear middle part of the passenger jeepney I was driving with such force that its rider driver was thrown off high in the air and dropped face down flat on the cemented boulevard, four of his front teeth scattered on the thoroughfare, he almost died. Police investigated the matter and although I tried to explain to the police that I had nothing to do with the accident, that the accident was caused by the motorcycle driver himself and no one else, I was surprised and frightened when the police charged me with reckless imprudence resulting to frustrated homicide and arrested me. I was incarcerated at the Manila City Jail pending the hearing of my case. That night while in jail I seemed to hear the voice of my mother loud and clear:

"My son, what you wanted to do is a mistake and childish;

it is hard to be driving the whole day for commission of a meager sum while running all kinds of risks, what if you run over a pedestrian by accident, you will be arrested and be charged in court; who will bail you out; how will you pay your lawyer? Lawyers are costly and court hearings run a long way. In the meantime who will feed your wife, your son, your family. My son the wiser thing to do is for you to go back to school, go to college and be a lawyer;

"Remember my son, people are born in this world not just 'to work to eat ' nor just 'to eat to work' but to do justice and fight evil as a tribute to honor and praise God Almighty.

"My son I wish you would go back to school, go to college, be a lawyer. I will pray for you son."

All through that night I did not sleep.. I kept telling myself, what if by mistake or ignorance or whatever reason the judge find me guilty as charged, even if I knew by myself I had nothing to do with the accident, and send me to prison to serve some years of prison term, then I will be sent to a "brigada" a Tagalog vernacular term to prison cell. A "brigada" or prison cellusually contain a hundred inmates.It has been the custom in prison to give a "pasalubong" a Tagalog vernacular term for "welcome" to a new inmate which means that the old inmates will each give the arriving "new" inmates a punch in the body. Considering the size of my body, I was thin and weak by nature, I am sure I will not survive the "pasalubong", so I was terribly frightened by the thought of it.

Actually "pasalubong" has long been prohibited by law, however the custom was apparently tolerated by prison officials as a deterrent for people to "behave" in fear of it. So I asked my mother to bail me out. After a day or two, I was told by my mother that she acted at once on my request to her to bail me out, so she requested our neighbor policeman Mr. Santos and his wife to accompany her (my mother) to the insurance company issuing bailbonds, so the three of them went to the Insurance Company at Dewey Boulevard to secure bailbond for me. However, the Insurance Company refused to issue the bailbond requested by my mother as she could not comply with the Insurance Company's requirement to give a title to a house and lot in Manila and suburbs to the Insurance Company as collateral for the bailbond so that if the "accused" in whose favor the bailbond was issued will abscond or will "run away" or will "jump bail", that is, will not appear at the hearing of his case, the Insurance Company may recover its damages from the colateral, -- that was the SOP (Standard Operating Procedure) of the insurance Company in issuing bailbonds.

I then realized how hard for a poor man to have a court case as he will be imprisoned at once pending hearing of his case as if already convicted, and so even if finally he gets acquitted he has already suffered the loss of years of his life in prison.

Desperate, I turned to prayer. I prayed hard day and night to the Good Lord, God Almighty to get me out of my miserable situation. "I had not done anything illegal, or against the law, I had not done anything wrong against my fellow being, yet I am in prison, I cried to God in my prayers. Please help me out, and I promise I will do what my mother asked me to do. I will go back to school, I will be a lawyer as she wish me to be -- but then, the more I will need Your help and guidance, Lord, so that if I win my case,. it must be because justice and truth demand it, and if I lose my case I lose it not because of my "kabobohan" (meaning, stupidity, or lack of knowledge or lack of skill) but because it will be "unfair and unjust" to win it.".Amen

Then one morning our neighbor-lawyer and owner of the jeepney I was driving for commission, the one involved in the accident, came to me in jail and told me the happy and unexpected news, as he said:

Neighbor- lawyer owner of the jeepney: "Virgilio, pack up to go home, I had convinced the motorcycle rider and victim to execute an affidavit, (i.e., sworn statement), clearing your name of any involve- ment in the accident inasmuch as you really had nothing to do with the accident and that he ought to be thankful to have survived the accident and was given by God another life to live so he should return the favor and show his gratitude by clearing your name, an innocent person suffering in jail because of his fault. On the basis of his affidavit clearing your involvement in the accident, the Fiscal moved for the withdrawal of the case against you. The judge approved the withdrawal of the case against you and "ordered" for your immediate release from detention. So you are now free. Come on, I will bring you home. Your mother has been waiting for you."

All I could say then was, "thank you Sir."

I then looked up and muttered a silent prayer, "Good Lord, this is a miracle, I thank you Lord God Almighty, Praise be Your Name Forever." Amen.

Chapter III

I Am A Lawyer

(Names* fictional/events factual)

Our neighbor-lawyer-owner of the passenger jeepney brought me home. He dropped me on our street a few steps from our house. While I was happily walking towards our house my childhood sweetheart, Bening who lived in the house of her married sister's house near our house rushed towards me from her house and blurted out,:

Bening: "Virgilio, I heard the insurance company refused to bail you out, how come you are here, did you escape? I realized I have no bright future with you, from now on, I am cutting our relationship, don't talk to me anymore, goodbye.", and before I could tell her I did not escape but I was legally released by the Judge, she had already walked away from me and out of my life

I continued walking towards our house as I told myself, "Funny I did not feel any heartache at all"

I knocked at the door of our house. My mother opened the door and we embraced each other. I told her, "I promise I will go back to school, I will be a lawyer, as you wish, Mother".

Years swiftly passed by unnoticed.

It was March 15, 1965, an unforgetable moment of my life,. We, my mother and I, attended the oath taking of new lawyers at the Supreme

Court of the Philippines. It was a an unforgetable moment in my life, March 15 1965.

Together with all the other new lawyers, with right hand raised up, I recited the Lawyer's Oath before the Supreme Court Justice designated to conduct the oath taking of the new lawyers. I recited with all solemnity the words:

LAWYER's OATH

I, Attorney Virgilio J. Santiago, do solemnly swear that I will maintain allegiance to the Republic of the Philippines, I will support it's Constitution and obey the laws as well as the legal orders of the duly constituted authorities therein; I will do no falsehood, nor consent to the doing of any in court; I will not wittingly or willingly promote or sue any groundless, false or unlawful suit, nor give aid nor consent to the same; I will delay no man for money or malice, and will conduct myself as a lawyer according to the best of my knowledge amd discretion with all good fidelity as well to the courts as to my clients; and I impose upon myself this voluntary obligation without any mental reservation or purpose of evasion. SO HELP ME GOD."

After the oath taking we, the new lawyers scribed our signatures opposite our names and our individual roll number in the big log book kept in and by the Supreme Court.

That was a solemn, memorable moment for every lawyer, for thenceforth, the lawyer is entitled to use the prefix "Atty." or "Attorney" before his name. No person, be he the riches, and/or high official of the government may use the prefix "Atty." or "Attorney" without his name being registered in the "log book" of the Supreme Court.

After the solemn memorable happy occassion, my mother and I went home and celebrated the happy and momentous event of my life. We ate pansit or noodles and bread, with hot chocolate for my mother and coffee, for me.

After the celebration, I took out my "karatula" a Tagalog vernacular for "signboard" with the following inscriptions:

****

Atty. Virgilio J. Santiago

Counsellor –at- Law	Trial Lawyer
Office Hours: 24 Hours	by: Appointment Only
Tel. No. (209) 957-0670	e-mail: vjsan51536@yahoo.com

We believe in: "Those who have less in life should have more in law"

*** "Nothing is impossible with God"

****

I attached my Signboard on the front door of our house

I made the sala or living room of our house my "law office" with the permission of my mother, by arranging the furnitures. I have my office table, my swivel chair in front of my office table, two chairs for visitors-client, sofa for companions of the visitors, or for those waiting for consultation or legal advice, and telephone on top of my table.

Every morning, I made it a habit to go to the courtrooms at Quezon City Hall in formal attire of "coat and tie "in color flesh with white shoes to observe the manner and conduct of old lawyers, of fiscals, and judges, and also witnesses in actual hearings. In doing so I imbibed the atmosphere of the court which is the battleground wherein cases are fought, win or lose. I found my habit a strategy not taught in the law schools. I have exposed myself to clients, and handled criminal and civil cases in the City Courts, Metropolitan City Courts, Courts of First Instance (later called the Regional Trial Courts) of Manila, Quezon City, Pasay, Pasig, Makati, Caloocan City, Malabon, Paranque, Las Pinas, Laguna, and Zamboanga City, to name some, and some Administrative Investigations conducted by the National Bureau of Investigation (NBI), the Congress of the Philippines.

Some rules of evidence worth memorizing by heart are:

(1) Privileged communication: An attorney cannot, without the consent of his client be examined as to any communication made by the client to him or his advice given thereon in the course of, or with a view to, professional employment, nor can an attorney's secretary, stenographer, or clerk, be examined without the consent

of the client and his employer concerning any fact the knowledge of which has been acqured in such capacity.

(2) An act or declaration made in the presence and within the hearing and observation of a party who does or says nothing when the act or declaration is such as naturally to call for action or comment if not true and when possible and proper for him to do so may be given in evidence against him.;

(3) The husband or the wife, during or after the marriage, cannot Be examined without the consent of the other as to any communication received in confidence by one from the other during the marriage except in a civil case by one against the other, or in a criminal case for a crime committed by one against the other or the latter's direct descendants or ascendants.

(4) "Evidence "is the means sanctioned by these rules (Rules on evidence, Rule 128, Rules of Court), of ascertaining in a judicial proceedings the truth respecting a matter of fact. So I acquired confidence necessary to handle tight situations and absurd conditions in courtrooms combat as in court a lawyer is all alone. Coaching not allowed, and usually, experience tell us who have come to know already, "coached argument" are usually "wrong in timing", "wrong in essence", or "not applicable", and were even "at times immaterial" or "irrelevant", and even "absurd and ridiculous".

Some lawyers I have talked to said they were bothered to accept criminal cases wherein the client had admitted the commission of the offense and found hard on their concience to fight it out as vigorous as if they were not told the truth, so they want my opinion on the matter. I had the same experience, and I resolved it thus—

One time, our neighbor Engr. Noli Castor *, (name fictional/event true), came to my office and asked me if I will accept to defend his son who admitted to him having committed the charge of "Murder"

I answered him, as follows:

Atty Santiago: Engr. Noli Castor, I am a lawyer. I was not a witness to whatever happened that resulted to your son being charged of "Murder". I cannot rely on the admission of your son. I do not know why your son was admitting the charge, who made him admit the charge, what made him admit the charge.

His telling you that he committed the charge was "hearsay" and not "admissible" in court.

Under the Constitution, the accused is "presumed to be innocent "and cannot be "compelled to be a witness against himself.".

Therefore I have no right to refuse to defend your son "just because he admitted the charge to you".

Anyway, Engineer Castor, the accusser has all the obligation "to prove the guilt of your son beyond reasonable doubt in accordance with the rules on evidence and procedure."

Engr. Noli Castor: So. You will accept to defend my son. Atty. Santiago?, he asked me.

Atty. Santiago: Of Course if you want me to defend your son -- but subject to my terms and condition.

Engr. Noli Castor: What condition, Atty. Santiago?

Atty. Santiago: First is payment of Acceptance fee, Fifty Thousand (Php 50,000) Pesos in your case; Second, appearance fee is Php 2,000 per appearance in court whether postponed or not;

Engr. Noli Castor: That's okay to me. So, I will give you now your Acceptance Fee in check;

Atty. Santiago: Please make it in cash- okay?

Eng. Noli Castor: Okay, I will bring the cash this evening. Thank you.

Atty. Santiago: When you bring the acceptance fee this evening we will go to the jail where your son is for "lawyer's interview and visit".

Engr. Noli Castor: It is nightime, can we do that?, he asked me.

Atty, Santiago: Well, we can insist that we be allowed - that is a lawyer's visit - Under Republic Act 7438 Sec. 4, (b) Penalty Clause, It is provided that, "Any person who obstructs, prevents, or prohibits any lawyer from visiting and conferring privately with a person arrested, detained or under custodial investigation at any hour of the day or in urgent cases, of the night, shall suffer the penalty of imprisonment of not less than 4 years nor more than 6 years and a fine of Four Thousand (P4,000) Pesos.

Engr. Noli Castor: Okay Thank you. See you then, Atty. Santiago. I looked up and said "Thank You Good Lord, God Almighty Praise be Your Name forever." Amen.

Before and after my court hearings, I always say –"Good Lord, God Almighty please let me win the case for Justice and truth must prevail. Please do not allow me to lose the case just because of my "kabobohan" (meaning, stupidity / lack of knowledge or lack of skill) but because truth and justice demand it.

This episode was included in the hope and wish that the lawyer and those who would want to be lawyers will strive to win their case not only for personal gain or glory but for truth and justice and to honor and glorify the Good Lord God Almighty.

Chapter IV

The 1 Million Pesos Qualified Theft Case

(*names fictional / incidents true and factual)

One day my gallivanting older brother, Kuya Henry came to the house with a companion he introduced as one Retired Colonel Magnalonso * II, as kuya Henry said:

Kuya Henry: I brought my friend Retired Colonel Magnalonso * II here as he want you Atty. Santiago (he always referred to me as Atty. Santiago. since I became a lawyer) to handle the defense of his son, Carlito Magnalonso III due for hearing before the Fiscal's office of Rizal at the Kapitolyo of Pasig, Rizal tomorrow at 2 o'clock

Col. Magnalonso II: That's right, Atty. Santiago, I asked your brother, Henry, my long time friend to accompany me to your office to ask you to handle the defense of my son Carlito Magnalonso III* who was charged by Retired Colonel Merito * of One Million Peso Qualified Theft of clothing materials. Col. Merito owns a tailoring shop doing uniform for the Philippine Army. My son Carlito was employed by Col. Merito as Chief Cutter of his tailoring shop. I and Col. Merito has a long misunderstanding and to get even with me he want to destroy the name of my son Carlito Magnalonso III and destroy my name also since we have the same name. Also by charging my son with this embarrassing case, my son could not get "police clearance" and "fiscal's clearance" necessary to get "visa to go to America to establish his own tailoring shop to service our "kababayan" there. I do not want to get other lawyers as I know Col. Merito to be a "corruptor". He might corrupt my son's lawyer to "sell" my son's case – As I trust your brother, I know I can trust you also. Just tell me how much you will charge me as your professional fee, I will pay as soon as the case is finished.

Atty Santiago: Well. as we want to be professional about this case, I will charge you acceptance fee - usually I charge 20% of the amount involved in the case, plus appearance fee of Php 200 for every appearance postponed or not, and 25% of whatever amount received by the client from the adverse party by way of amicable setlement or by decision -- however considering your friendship with my brother Kuya Henry, I will ask you to pay me acceptance fee of Twenty Thousand (Php 20,000) Pesos only never mind the appearance fee But I wil charge you also 25% of whatever amount you will receive from Col. Merito* by way of amicable settlement or by decision. Is that okay with you, Col. Magnalonso. Sir?

Col. Magnalonso: "Well that's okay with me – Thank you for charging me 2% only of the amount of Php 1 Million peso involved in the case, Atty. Santiago ", and he laughed;

Then Col. Magnalonzo continued:

Col. Magnalonzo: "By the way, Atty. Santiago, what do you mean by you will charge me '25% of whatever amount I will receive from Col. Merito by way of amicable settlement or decision'?"--

Atty. Santiago: Ah, there are times when a complainant or plaintiff is "ordered by the Court" to pay the defendant or accused certain amount of penalty for filing an unjust or unlawful case so the counsel or lawyer of the defendant or accused must be compensated also by the client for that particular benefit is that not right, Col. Magnalonso, Sir?

Col. Magnalonso: That will be nice if I will be paid by Col. Merito on that premise, I will be glad to pay Atty, Santiago extra 25% of the amount he pays me. Anyway, my son and I will pick you up at 1 o'clock tomorrow here at your office., then. We will go together to the Fiscal'a office at 'Kapitolyo' Okay?

Atty Santiago: By the way, Col. Magnalonso, Were you copy furnished of the affidavit-complaint and other papers in the case by Col. Merito?

Col. Magnalonso handed to me the affidavit-complaint of Col. Merito as he said:

Col. Magnalonso: I received the "subpoena" for my son to appear at the office of the fiscal at Kapitolyo at Pasig, Rizal, tomorrow at 2 o'clock for the hearing of the complaint of Col. Merito of One Million Pesos Qualified Theft against him; Attachd to the subpoena was the Affidavit-Complaint of Col. Merito. That's all I received.

Atty. Santiago: Okay then, I will just wait for you here at my office.

"Acceptance fee is supposed to be paid upon acceptance of the case" I said to myself, it's okay, this case was an exception.

I studied the Affidavit-Complaint of Col. Merito. I read and reread, once, twice, and thrice the affidavit, I could not find any element of the crime of Qualified Theft in it.

That night I restudied the affidavit-complaint of Col. Merito. There was really no element of Qualified Theft in it.

The next day, exactly one o'clock in the afternoon, I was already ready in coat and tie, waiting for my clients Carlito* Magnalonso II and III and as soon as they arrived I bid goodbye to my mother.

We rode in the Hillman "Hunter" car air-conditioned, well tuned- up, road-worthy "fully loaded" newly painted, with radio and new tires, of Col. Magnalonzo.

We reached the Kapitolyo of Rizal at Pasig, Rizal, about 1:30 o'clock, so we roamed around the area of the fiscal's office, when I chanced to meet Atty. Soc Pena, one of my classmates at the Manuel L. Quezon Law School (now Manuel L. Quezon College of Law), So we greeted each other,:

Atty. Pena: How are you doing, Atty. Santiago. Long time no see. What brought you to Kapitolyo of Rizal? He asked me.

Atty. Santiago: I have here my clients Col. Magnalonso, and his son, we are to appear at a Qualified Theft case at Room 234. What about you, Panero, where's your hearing? I asked him.

Atty. Pena: I also have a hearing there, I see it's about 2 o'clock already, I will have to go to the restroom first, Panero. Okay, see you -- and he ran off.

Atty. Pena rushed to the restroom, while I, Magnalonso II and III went on our way to Room 234.

Magnalonzo II and III, and I entered Room 234 at exactly 2 o'clock.

"The complainant Col. Merito* and his lawyer were inside already ", Magnalonso II whispered to me.

Atty. Soc Pena enterd the room and greeted everybody good afternoon.

Fiscal Pena: Good afternoon everybody. First case, Col. Merito, complainant for One Million Peso Qualified Theft, versus Carlito Magnalonso, III, Respondent, --

Col. Merito: Complainant, Col, Merito,* present., Mr. Fiscal. I have here my counsel.

Atty. Don Bueno,*: Counsel for Col. Merito, Mr. Fiscal, we are submitting the Affidavit-Complaint of Col. Merito.

Atty. Santiago: Atty. Santiago, respectfully appearing as counsel for respondent, Carlito Magnalonso III, Mr. Fiscal.

Fiscal Soc Pena*: Complainant Col. Merito, whose signature is this signature on the bottom page of this Affisavit- Complaint consisting of one (1) page?

Col. Merito: My signature, Mr. Fiscal.

Fiscal: Alright, please raise your right hand, do you swear that the contents of this affidavit -complaint are true and correct and of your own personal knowledge, So help you God, Complainant Col. Merito?

Col. Merito: Yes Mr. Fiscal.

Fiscal: Atty. Santiago here is a duplicate original copy of the affiavit-complaint of Complainant Col. Merito, any comment,? observation or cross-examination for respondent?

Atty. Santiago: With the kind indulgence of the Honorable Fiscal., Mr. Complainant Col. Merito, will you kindly read your Affidavit-Complaint and tell us if there is any change you would like to make in it, or delete from it, or alter in it or amend in it, after you have sworn on it?

Col. Merito: What I have said in my Affidavit-Complaint were true and correct, there 's nothing I will change on it, or alter in it, or amend in it, or delete from it. Everything I have said on it stay.

Atty. Santiago: Nullum Crimen, Nullum poena; Cine lege, cine pena -- Mr. Fiscal -- We respectfully move to Dismiss the complaint of Complainant Col. Merito against respondent Carlito Magnalonso, III, on the following legal grounds:

1. The Affidavit -Complaint of Complainant Col. Merito revealed (a) That Col. Merito did not see personally the respondent, Carlito Magnalonso III took for his personal gain, any piece of clothing material, away from the tailoring shop to the damage and prejudice of the tailoring shop and/or Col. Merito; (b) That no witness had seen respondent Carlito Magnalonso III, took for his personal gain any piece of clothing material away from the tailoring shop to the damage and prejudice of the tailoring shop and/or Col. Merito.; (c) That no special trust and confidence was reposed on respondent Carlito Magnalonso III, by Col. Merito as to enable Carlito Magnalonso III, to take advantage to carry and take away clothing material of the tailoring shop for his personal gain and benefit to the damage and prejudice of the tailoring shop and/or Col. Merito. and (d) That no damage or prejudice was alleged in the affidavit-complaint; (e) That no inventory of the clothing materials was alleged and exhibited to show that there was in fact loss of clothing materials.

2) That were the allegations of the accusation were in themselves insufficient to show that facts and circumstances exist as to engender a well founded belief that a crime has been committed and that the respondent was probably guilty thereof and should be held for trial, the accusation should and must be dismissed as no proof is necessary to controvert it. Res ipsa loquitur, the thing speaks for itself, applies—

As was substantially stated by the Honorable Supreme Court,:

-The prosecuting officer is the representative not of an ordinary party to a controversy but of a sovereignty whose obligation to govern impartially is as compelling as its obligation to govern at all, and whose interest therefore in a criminal prosecution is not that it shall win a case but that justice shall be done. As such he is in a peculiar and very definite sense the servant of the law, the two fold aim of which is that guilt shall not escape nor innocense suffer. He may prosecute with earnestness and vigor, indeed he should do so, but while he may strike hard blows he is not at liberty to strike foul ones. It is as much his duty to refrain from methods calculated to produce a wrongful conviction as it is to use every legitimate means to bring about a just one. -

Wherefore premises considered we move once again to Dismiss the complaint.

After the Fiscal read, once, twice and reread again the Affidavit-Complaint of Col. Merito, the Fiscal right then and there resolved to Dismiss the case and declared:

Fiscal: For lack of sufficient facts and circumstances tending to engender a well founded belief that the crime of Qualified Theft had been committed and that the respondent Carlito Magnalonso III, was probably guilty thereof and should be held for trial, the complaint is hereby Dismissed.

Atty. Bueno: Motion for reconsideration Mr. Fiscal -- we can present other witnesses to --

Fiscal: Panero, you cannot present other witness to controvert the allegations of the complainant That's against procedure. Motion for reconsideration denied. Complaint Dismissed.

Complainant Col. Merito rushed out of the Fiscal's room with face red with anger.

I looked at the Fiscal, we smiled to each other.

I looked up and uttered: "Thank You God Almighty, Praise be Your Name forever."

Father and son Carlito Magnalonso II and III embraced each other, as Col. Magnalonso whispered to me:

Col. Magnalonso II: Atty. Santiago, I never thought my son's case will end today in our favor this early, I did not bring your acceptance fee Atty. Santiago as I did not think we could win this case so swiftly, and now that the case of my son has been dismissed I will give all my money to him so he can get "Visa" and "passport" to go to America and start his tailoring business there. But don't worry, I will pay now your acceptance fee -- you see the "Hillman –Hunter car" the one we used coming here at the Fscal's office today, you see how road-worthy it was, newly painted, new tires, air-conditioned, with radio. You can use it going to and fro your court hearings. I will give it to you as your acceptance fee, will you accept it?

Atty. Santiago: Of Course I will, Col. Magnalonso II, if that's what you want. Let us go to the Land Transportation Office and transfer it to my name, Okay?

Col. Magnalonso II: Okay, Let's go.

So that day, I went home riding my own car, Hillman "Hunter" Airconditioned, with radio, new tires, newly painted, road-worthy, well tuned-up -- I can use for going to and fro my court hearings.

My mother's words again flashed to my mind "lawyers are compensated not only with 'treasure, pleasure and honor, but more, the right to right a wrong' "

I looked up and said once more: "Thank You Lord God Almighty for the car you gave me:".

Some years later, Col. Magnalonso called me up and told me his son had invited him to come to America as "tourist" with airline ticket to and fro and with Bank Deposit of One Million Pesos (Php 1,000,000) in his name as per "tourist visa requirment".

How happy was the old man..

I looked up and said softly: "Thank You God Almighty, Praise be Your Name forever. Amen."

Chapter V

A Little Learning Is A Dangerous Thing

(Names* fictional/incidents factual)

One Sunday morning, I have just arrived from church and was relaxing in my Law Office in our house, when one Dr. Felo Roman* as per his self-introduction came to the office and said:

Dr. Roman: Good Morning, Atty. Santiago, I am Doctor Roman, I lived down your street, I came over to seek your legal advice.

So, I answered him, thus:

Atty. Santiago: Yes Dr. Roman, what's your legal problem?. But before we continue, Dr. Roman, I charge consultation fee.,. for legal advice, --

Dr. Roman: Its okay with me, Atty. Santiago, how much is your consultation fee, for legal advice?

Atty. Santiago: Only Php 2,000 for simple legal questions and problems., Dr. Roman.

Dr. Roman: Okay, Atty. Santiago -

Atty. Santiago: Alright, what's your legal problem, please --

Dr. Roman: I have a car, brand new car, I had it insured against all damages, third party and own damage insurance, that is, when the car is damage the insurance pays whether of my own fault or anybody's fault, that was the explanation of the insurance agent - so to secure myself from whatever road risks, I insured my car, with third party and own damage coverage and paid my premiums.

Atty. Santiago: That was the right thing to do. So what happened if any, Dr. Roman?

Dr. Roman: You know Atty. Santiago, I am a doctor, I also teach English I and II in a known University in Manila, so I know my English.

Atty. Santiago: Please continue Dr. Roman, what happened if any?

Dr. Roman: Last June 13 this year while I was driving to Ilocos to answer a "VIP", "Very Important Patient" call, on a curve of the National Highway, my tire slipped and my brand new car crushed head on the adobe fence of ex- Senator Uy* causing the fence to crumble and my brand new car a total wreck. The guards and bodyguards of ex-senator Uy rushed outside with their long and short guns aiming at me.

Atty. Santiago: That's terrible accident. What happend to you, Dr. Roman, did you suffer any injuries? I asked him.

Dr. Roman: Luckily, my brand new car had an Air-bag installed in it for such an accudent. It saved me from injuries and maybe death.

Atty. Santiago: Then what happened next?

I asked him.

Dr. Roman: I was brought to the house where I was met by ex-Senator Uy*. After some amenities, the Senator asked me what I intend to to do with his fence which crumbled. I looked around me and saw his "Pitbull Dogs" tutored to attack at the snap of his finger, and some bodyguards with long firearms ready at his command, so,.I had to admit my liability, and said I will pay whatever damage he may suffer from the accident. The Senator ordered his secretary-lawyer to type right then and there a written compromise agreement wherein was stated that I, Dr. Roman* will pay ex Senator Uy* the sum of Fifty Thousand (Php 50,000) on or before June 30 1967, without necessity of demand, as damages I caused to the "adobe fence" of his house at Pangasinan,; That failure on my part to pay my acknowledged obligation, will cause Senator Uy to file an action for collection of a plain and valid obligation and I will be obliged to pay an agreed Attorney's fee of One Hiundred Thousand (Php 100,000) Pesos as penalty in favor of Senator Uy*., without necessity of demand, also.,

'"That's my legal problem, Atty. Santiago'". Sighed Dr. Roman. "

Atty. Santiago: So you will have to face Senator Uy in court. Prove that the compromise agreement was not voluntarily entered by you because of "duress". Get a good, fighting lawyer., That's my advise,.

By the way, why don't you write your Insurance to pay the damage of Senator Uy*, anyway you were insured with "Third Party Liability, I asked Dr. Roman.

Dr. Roman answered: I did that. I wrote the Insurance asking them to pay the damages of Senator Uy and also to replace my total wrecked brand new car of the same brand and model.

Atty. Santiago: That's good. Who wrote the letter of demand, when, what's the reply of the Insurance, I asked Dr. Roman.

Dr. Roman, with sad face answered:

Dr. Roman: The Insurance Company Denied my claim.

Atty. Santiago: Why, what's their reason, I asked Dr. Roman.?

Dr. Roman: The Insurance said because the accident happened during the time of Typhoon Sendang, the Insurance will not pay the claim being one of the "excepted risks". Is that right, Atty. Santiago?

Atty. Santiago: Well if that was in the Policy of Insurance, then they were right to refuse your claim., I told him point blank. But of course, all claim, your claim and the claim of basis of "denial" of the insurance must be proved by evidence.

Dr. Roman: What shall I do, then, Atty. Santiago?;

Atty. Santiago: Actually the problem was the "Letter of Demand "to the Insurance, who wrote that letter,?

Dr. Roman: Well, Atty. Santiago as I have told you already, I am teaching English -- I wrote that letter because it was just a simple notice to the Insurance, about an accident and a car insured by them, they should pay, is it not Atty. Santiago?

Atty. Santiago: Actually, I am sorry to say, but that's the begining of the problem, it was written in plain good English, but without consideration of the legal implications -- like the accident happening during the typhoon which exempts an insurance from risk undertaken by it during such event.. detailed in the policy.

Dr. Roman: So what can we do now, Atty. Santiago?

Atty. Santiago: You do two things, first: Get back your letter of demand; second: Get a good, fighting lawyer to defend you from the oncoming suit of ex-Senator Uy.

Dr. Roman: I will try to get back the letter; And I want you Atty. Santiago to defend me from the suit of ex-Senator Uy -- will that be okay with you, Atty. Santiago?

Atty. Santiago: That's okay to me, but for that I will I charge acceptance fee, 20% of Php 150,000, that's Php 30,000 plus Php 200 per appearance for every hearing whether postponed or not, plus Attorney's fee of 25% of whatever amount client receive from adverse party by court decision or amicable settlement,;

Dr. Roman: What's that 25% attorney's fee?

Atty. Santiago: There are times when the complainant or adverse party files a complaint which turn out to be unlawful or improper so the court gives a verdict in favor of the defendant with damages say Php 500,000 or 'milllion Pesos, of course, the lawyer for the defendant should be compensated for that, is it not?

Dr. Roman: That's good to hear. So not every complainant is awarded its complaint.?

Atty. Santiago: Of Course.

Dr. Roman: Okay, I will give you your Acceptance fee, Php 30,000.

Soon after the 30th day of June passed Senator Uy by counsel filed collection suit for sum of money Fifty Thousand (Php 50,000) Pesos actual damages for the "adobe wall" of his house at Pangasinan which crumbled caused by alleged reckless driving of Dr. Felo Roman on 13th[th] day of June 1967 plus attorney's fees One Hundred Thousand (Php 100,000) Pesos as agreed penalty in the Compromise Agreement, attached to the Complaint plus moral damages Five Hundred Thousand (Php 500,000) Pesos to teach Defendant Dr. Felo Roman to abide by his commitment and legal obligation especially when the party to the agreement is a person who was a former Senator and ought to be respected.

Within fifteen (15) days after summons was served to Defendant Dr. Felo Roman, I filed Answer to the Complaint of ex-Senator Uy that the "Compromise Agreement "attached to the Complaint was void as defendant Dr. Felo Roman was "under Duress" at the time he signed it; that the "incident" was an accident and the allegation that it was caused by the "reckless driving" of defendant Dr. Felo Roman was a conclusion at law without basis in fact and in law and besmirched the reputation and personality of Dr. Felo Roman as a "reckless" person; that the car of Dr. Felo Roman was insured against Third Party Liability with premium duly paid and valid; that a claim for insurance payment of the damages of Plaintiff ex-Senator s "Adobe Wall" for Fifty Thousand (P50,000) has been filed by Dr. Felo Roman as soon as a day or two after the accident and if only the Insurance Company has paid its insurance obligation, the parties to the instant case of collection of money should not have been inconvenienced Dr. Felo Roman, wherefore, the defendant Dr, Felo Roman hereby incorporate his allegations in this Answer as he hereby complain against the Insurance Company by way of Third-Party Complaint and alleges that the Insurance Company has by its Insurance Policy duly issued in favor of Dr. Felo Roman is under obligation to pay Honorable Ex-Senator Uy actual damage of Fifty Thousand (Php 50,000) for the "Adobe Wall" of his house at Pangasinan, and whatever damages may be awarded him by virtue of the delay of the Insurance Company to fulfill its duty under the terms of insurance undertaken by it in favor of the herein defendant. And to replace the wrecked car of insured Dr. Felo Roman with another car of the same model and brand in lieu of the totally wrecked car.

That we pray for such other relief as may be just and equitable in the premises.

The Answer as well as the Third-Party Complaint against the Defendant Insurance Company has been filed and up to present time of this writing still on the hearing stage at Pangasinan Court of First Instance (now Regiomal Trial Court of Pangasinan).

The morale of the episode is that not every complainant wins his case.

I looked up and fervently prayed: Thank you Lord. God Almighty, Praise be Your Name Forever. Amen.

Chapter VI

The "King Solomon Defense" in The Laundry Girl Case

(Name * fictional, but events true)

One day, I was taking merienda at the VIP Coffee Shop of the VIP Hotel at Dewey Boulevard, when I read in the newspaper that Eleuterio Adevoso, famous guerilla leader during the Japanese invasion of the Philippines was at the Lobby of the VIP Building to launch his "Memories of Wartime" written by himself, part of which exciting book was the heroic "saving of the life of then an 'unknown poor man from Lubao' who was due for execution by a squad of Japanese soldiers in an unknown cemetery when Eleuterio Adevoso the young Guerilla leader and his troop swoop down on the Japanese soldiers and killed them all. The "poor man from Lubao" was Diosdado Macapagal, destined to become President of the Republic of the Philippines". Adevoso became Administrator of the "Emergency Employment Agency, and later, became one of the "key Secretaries" of President Diosdado Macapagal.

Feeling patriotic, I thought of going to the lobby to catch a glimpse of the "big man hero". It was at that point in time that I noticed a fine old man about 65 years of age, seated on the table near mine, looking at me, so I smiled at him and I said, "Good Afternoon" Sir, to show that I was friendly and also a gentleman. I showed him respect as he also look friendly, respectable, and much older than I was. I was then about 32 years old only.

The fine old man greeted me also as he said:

"Good Afternoon to you also, young man, I think you are a lawyer, am I correct?", he asked, me.

Atty. Santiago: Yes Sir, I am Atty. Virgilio J. Santiago, Sir., I answered

He extended his hand and we shook hands in handshake, as. he said:

Mr, Teng: I am Mr. Teng.* I am in Insurance business, I have my office at the fourth floor. I see you were reading the article on Mr. Adevoso, he was a courageous anti - Japanese guerilla during the war. But now no more, Japanese and Philippines friends, we do business with each other. I served under him during the war.

Atty. Santiago: O, is that so, then I might be able to meet him through you, Mr. Teng.

Mr. Teng: That I will do gladly. By the way, Atty. Santiago, My wife would like to obtain the services of a young girl about l7 years old as family "lavandera", laundry girl. This young girl was serving as family laundry girl of another family. When her "Amo" or woman boss learned that this young girl intended to change employment and would like to go to my Mrs., and be our family laundry girl, her woman boss charged her with "Qualified Theft" and had her jailed.

Mr. Teng heaved a deep sigh—

Atty. Santiago: That was pitiful, I commented--

Mr. Teng: Her case is now pending with the court of Judge Pamaran, of Manila City. Her case was scheduled for hearing tomorrow at 2:00 o'clock in the afternoon. The last time it was postponed for lack of witnesses for the prosecution. Her lawyer appointed by the court as "Counsel de Officio" did not object to the postponement so it was re- scheduled for tomorrow. Since she is under custody of the court for failure to file bail, she is prejudiced every time her case is postponed. I want to change her counsel to give her a better fighting chance. I wonder if you can help her, I will pay your attorney's fees, how much do you charge for this kind of case?

Atty. Santiago: Well, as you are helping her, then I might also help her. Ordinarily I charge Acceptance fee of Ten Thousand (PHp 10,000) Pesos for this kind of criminal case as this has imprisonment of from 8 to 12 years, but considering that both of us are just helping her, I will then accept it for Two Thousand (Php 2,000) Pesos only, never mind the appearance fees.

At that time, year 1968, the regular charge of ordinary lawyer as acceptance fee for serious offenses was Ten Thousand (Php 10,000) Pesos and One Hundred (Php 100) Pesos for appearance fee per hearing, postponed or not postponed as long as the lawyer appear in court.

Mr. Teng: That was kind of you, Atty, Santiago –

Then he pulled his wallet and paid me Two Thousand (Php. 2,000) Pesos as acceptance fee,. while saying:

Mr. Teng: Tomorrow at 2:00 o'clock my Mrs and I will attend her scheduled hearing, I wish you could prevent another postponement as they are using it to prolong her unjust agony. Her name is "Antonia Dela Cruz". Okay, see you there, Atty. Santiago' I will still go to my office at the Fourth Floor..

I smiled at him while he stood up, I said:

Atty. Santiago: Here is your receipt, in my handwriting Sir. "Received from Mr. Teng Cash Two Thousand (2,000) Pesos as "Acceptance Fee for People vs. Antonia Dela Cruz, pending with the Court of Frist Instance of Manila, pre sided by Judge Pamaran, Sgd Atty. Virgilio J. Santiago June 25 1968. Thank you for trusting me, Sir.

And I handed to Mr. Teng his receipt.

About 1 PM the next day I was already at the Court of First Instance of Manila, Presided by Hon. Judge Pamaran (some years later, Judge Pamaran became Justice of Sandigan Bayan) office of the Clerk of Court. I requested for copy of the Information and read the "record of the case" "People of the Philippines versus Antonia Dela Cruz *, Criminal Case No. --------------- For Qualified Theft. The case has been scheduled for hearing twice but postponed at the instance of the prosecution without objection of the defense.

At 1:30 PM I entered the Courtroom of Judge Pamaran and greeted Mr. Teng and his wife, Dona Margarita Teng. Mr. Teng had already informed the accused Antonia Dela Cruz that she will be represented by Atty. Santiago, her new counsel.

At exactly 2:00 o'clock, Judge Pamaran entered the Courtroom, and soon thereafter, the Clerk of Court called the cases scheduled for hearing for that day.

Clerk of Court: People of the Philippines versus Antonia Dela Cruz, accused, Criminal Case No................. for Qualified Theft.

I at once stood up and entered my appearance, and said:

Atty. Santiago: Good Afternoon, Your Honor, I am Atty. Virgilio J. Santiago, respectfully appearing as "Counsel de Parte ' for accused Antonia Dela Cruz. We are ready.

Court: The Counsel de Officio appointed by the Court for the accused is hereby relieved as there is a new Counsel de Parte. Proceed Fiscal.

Fiscal: We are calling our first witness, PO1 Lito Anzures*, arresting officer, Manila Police Department. Station No. 2.

No PO1 Lito Anzures came forward, so the Fiscal manifested:

Fiscal: It appears Your Honor that our witness, PO1 Lito Anzures is not in court, we will be constrained to ask for a resetting of the hearing of the case.

At that point I I loudly voiced out my "objection",:

Atty. Santiago: "Objection" Your Honor please, it appears from the "records" of this case Your Honor, that this case had been postponed twice already at the "instance" of the prosecution. The accused Your Honor is a detention prisoner as she could not avail of her right to bail due to financial restraint, so much so that every time the prosecution reset the case for another date the "right of the accused to "speedy trial" is unduly violated.. Today's hearing will be the third time for the prosecution to present its evidence, if the prosecution cannot proceed with its obligation to prove the 'Guilt of the accused beyond reasonable doubt' then it is but just and proper upon motion of the accused through this representation to demand the "dismissal of the case against the accused for Non Prosequi".

We respectfully move to Dismiss the Case against the accused for "Non Prosequi". Thank You Your Honor..

Fiscal: The prosecution has the privilege as who to present among its witnesses to effectively prosecute its case, and had determined to present first the arresting officer, who for unknown reasons was not present in court today so we will request for a resetting of the hearing Your Honor.

Atty. Santiago: Your Honor, while the prosecution has the privilege to determine who to present first among its witnesses, it should be exercised in a manner not to violate the right of the accused. 'Sic utere tuo ut alienum non laedas' meaning, so use your property in a manner not to damage another. Also, under the law, "every person must in the exercise of his rights and in the performance of his duty act with justice, give everyone his due and oberve honesty and good faith". And more than all of these, the accused has the Constitutional guarantee to "speedy trial". So, if the Prosecution cannot prosecute the accused for lack of witnesses, that is its problem, but the accused should as a matter of right be released and the case against her "dismissed" in respect of the Constitution which is the highest law of the land.. We reiterate our Motion to Dismiss the case against the accused for "Non Prosequi" Your Honor.

Court: That's correct, If the prosecution could not proceed today, as per motion of the defense, this Court will "dismiss the case".

Fiscal: Alright we call the complainant Lorna Sy as our first witness.

A white skinned Chinese mestiza, a litle plump, approached the witness stand.

Court: Swear the witness, Ms Clerk of Court.

Clerk of Court: Ms. Witness, state your name, address, age, status and other personal circumstances—

Witness: I am Lorna Sy, married, residing at.................,housewife. Complainant in this case against accused Antonia Dela Cruz.

Clerk of Court: Mrs. Witness kindly raise your right hand and swear, "Do you swear to tell the truth, the whole truth and nothing but the truth in this case, so help you God?

Witness Mrs. Lorna Sy: I do, Madam.

Clerk of Court: Your witness, Fiscal.

Fiscal: Your Honor, we are presenting the witness to prove that she is the complainant in this case, that she can identify the accused in this case, that the accused stole money of the witness; that she was the one who called for the police to have the accused arrested and such other matters as may be relevant to this case

Court: Any objection or comment to the purpose, Atty. Santiago?

Atty. Santiago: None for the moment Your Honor, we reserve our right to object to "improper", "irrelevant", "Immaterial" "misleading" and such other "offensive questions "unfair to the accused".

Court: Proceed, Fiscal.

Fiscal: Mrs. Witness, are you the same Lorna Sy, the complainant in this case of Qualified Theft against accused Antonia Dela Cruz.?

Witness: I am sir.

Fiscal: Do you remember having executed an Affidavit-Complaint in connnection with this case, Mrs. Witness?

Witness: Yes, Sir.

Fiscal: Showing you this Affidavit- Complaint of one Lorna Sy against Antonia Dela Cruz for stealing Fifty pieces of one peso Coin with "Tamaraw emblem" signed "Lorna Sy" on top of the typewritten name Lorna Sy at the bottom of the page what relation has this affidavit-complaint with the affidavit complaint you said you executed in relation with this case,, Mrs. Witness?

Witness: That was my Affidavit-Complaint I executed in relation with this case, Sir.

Fiscal "Mrs. Witness, whose signature was that on top of the typewritten name Lorna Sy at the bottom of this Affidavit-Complaint?

Witness: My signaature, Sir.

Fiscal: Mrs. Witness do you affirm and confirm the truthfulness of everything in this Affidavit-Complaint as your personal knowledge?

Witness: I do, Sir.

Fiscal: We request the Affidavit - Complaint be marked as Exhibit "A" and the signature on top of the typewriten name Lorna Sy as Exhibit "A-1" and the name of Antonia Dela Cruz as Exhibit A-2 and the Fifty pieces in one peso coin with Tamaraw Emblem be marked as Exhibit "A- 3" all exhibits for the Prosecution.

Fiscal: Mrs. Witness Lorna Sy, will you look around and see

If the person you said stole money from you is in Court?

I at once stood up and voiced out a loud "Objection".

Atty. Santiago: Objection Your Honor, "Misleading and vague"

The question of the Fiscal as to the amount must be definite, as it is the question gives any amount which is not so in the Affidavit Complaint which was the basis of the "Information".

Court: Fiscal rephrase your question make the amount definite.

Fiscal: Mrs Witness kindly look around and point to the person whom you said stole fifty pieces of one peso coin with "Tamaraw Emblem" from you?

Witness: There she is, pointing to the accused.

Clerk of Court: The person pointed to by the accused, please stand up and tell this Court your name.

Accused: I am Antonia Dela Cruz, Madam.

Fiscal: That's all with the Witness, Your Honor.

Court: Any Cross Examination for the defense, Atty. Santiago?

Atty. Santiago: With the kind indulgence of the Honorable Court.

Court: Proceed.

Atty. Santiago: Mrs. Witness, please look over your Affidavit-Complaint, a duplicate original was issued to me by the Clerk of Court. Now, after looking over your Affidavit- Complaint, is there anything you want to change, delete or add to your Affidavit-Complaint, after you have sworn on it?

Witness: Nothing, Sir. They were all true and correct.

Atty. Santiago: Mrs. Witness, how long had the accused been your laundry girl? One year, two years?

Witness: More than 11 months. By December will be one year already. But she told me she wanted to go home to her province already by December.

Atty. Santiago: How much do you pay her per month?

Witness: I pay her Thirty (Php30) Pesos per month. That 's our contract. Thirty Pesos per month for one year, renewable after one year.

Atty. Santiago: Do you like the way she worked for you, Mrs. Witness?

Witness: Well she was okay.

Atty. Santiago: How do you pay her – in Cash, in peso bills, or in coins? What denominations?

Mrs. Witness: I pay her in 30 pieces one peso coin with tamaraw emblem -- Sir;

Atty. Santiago: Did Antonia Dela Cruz help in the kitchen?

Witness: She cooks well.

Atty. Santiago: Did Antonia help in cleaning the house?

Witness: Well she clean the house, good.

Atty. Santiago: Did Antonia clean the garage, Mrs. Witness?

Witness: My Mister come home about 11 PM everynight, Antonia clean the garage before sleeping.

Atty. Santiago: Mrs. Witness did Antonia clean the bathroom?

Witness: Yes, she also clean the bathroom.

Atty. Santiago: Did Antonia pay board and lodging?

Witness: No. Free board and lodging, that was in our contract.

Atty. Santiago: Aside from Antonia, your laundry girl, do you have other helper in the house, Mrs. Witness

Witness: No more other helper. Antonia was enough.

Atty. Santiago: Mrs. Witness, was there any occassion when Antonia asked for a raise of her pay?

Witness: No. She never asked me for a raise.

Atty. Santiago: Was there any time when Antonia went out of your house,

Witness: She never asked me permission to go out of the house.

Atty. Santiago: Mrs. Witness, so for 11 months Antonia had not gone out of your house, is that correct?

Witness: I had the key she cannot go out. She never asked permission to go out.

Atty. Santiago: Did Antonia had any visitor, Mra. Witness?

Mrs. Witness: No visitor for 11 months.

Atty. Santiago: When Antonia told you she want to go home to her province at the end of the contract, you told her she cannot go home as you will have no helper, correct?

Mrs. Witness: I told her, no, cannot go home, I have no helper here. I told her, I will give her raise of 10 Pesos per month make her wage P40 per month, but she still refused and insisted she will go home.

Atty. Santiago: So you got irritated at her, and told her you will send her to jail, if she insist on going home. that was what you told her is it not?

Witness: No, I did not tell her that..

Atty. Santiago: Of course you did, Mrs. Witness, as a matter of fact when after some weeks Antonia asked you to permit her to go home at the end of December this year, you called the police and complained against her for "stealing" your fifty pieces of one peso coin with Tamaraw Emblem", so the police took what you said as "Gospel" truth and arrested Antonia.

Mrs. Witness: That was the truth., Sir. The police found fifty pieces of one peso coin with Tamaraw Emblem inside her Talcum baby powder plastic container inside her "Tampipi" or "bamboo suitcase" (suitcase made of bamboo used to hold clothes of people coming from the province).

Atty. Santiago: You said in your Affidavit-Complaint, Mrs. Witness, "I placed my fifty pieces one peso coin with Tamaraw Emblem on top of my dresser cabinet when I took my bath. When I finished my bath, the coins were not there anymore. There were only two persons in the house at that time, myself and Antonia. I peeped into the room of Antonia, and saw her place my coins inside a talcum baby powder plastic container."

Now, Mrs. Witness, nobody saw who took your fifty pieces one peso coin with Tamaraw Emblem. You did not see who took your fifty pieces one peso coin with Tamaraw Emblem. Correct Mrs. Witness?

Mrs. Witness: Correct Sir.

Atty. Santiago: Even the police who arrested accused Antonia did not see who took the fifty pieces of one peso coins, correct, Mrs. Witness?

Mrs. Witness: Correct, Sir.

Atty. Santiago: The police arrested Antonia the accused on your allegsation that as there were only two of you in the house, you and Antonia, and as you claimed that you left your fifty pieces one peso coin with Tamaraw Emblem on top of your dresser when you took your bath and after you finished your bath they were not there anymore;, that when you peeped inside the room of Antonia you saw her placing your coins inside the Talcum plastic baby powder container that was what you said in your Affidavit-Complaint, correct, Mrs. Witness?

Mrs. Witness: Correct Sir.

Atty. Santiago: Now, let us see what the Talcum plastic baby powder container will say -- Your Honor, may we see the Talcum Baby Powder plastic container please.;

Court: Ms Clerk Of Court, please bring the Talcum Baby Powder plastic container here.

Clerk Of Court: Here is the Talcum Baby Powder plastic container, Your Honor.

The Clerk of Court placed the talcum baby powder plastic container on top of the table of Judge Pamaran.

Atty. Santiago: Mrs. Witness, is this the "Talcum Baby Powder plastic container of Antonia Dela Cruz, confiscated by the police when they arrested her?

Mrs. Witness: Yes Sir.

Atty. Santiago: I am opening now the plastic container, Your Honor and I am taking one piece of one peso coin with tamaraw emblem and I am showing it to the Witness: Mrs. Witness, what do you see about this coin?

Mrs. Witness: One Peso coin with Tamaraw Emblem Sir.

Atty. Santiago: I am showing to the Honorable Court the One Peso coin with tamaraw emblem, and I ask Mrs. Witness: Mrs witness was there any sign or name in it that will identify as to who it belongs to?

Mrs. Witness: None Sir.

I again took one coin from the plastic container, showed it to the witness and asked her "Mrs. Witness was there any sign or name in it that will identify as to who it belongs to?" and got the same answer from the witness, "none, sir." This process I made up to the fiftieth piece of one peso coin with 'Tamaraw Emblem' and got the same answer "none, sir" from the witness.

I then respectfully moved to dismiss the case against the accused, as I said:

"Your Honor, we, respectfully move to dismiss the case against accused Antonia Dela Cruz, on the following legal grounds:

(1) That there was no one who saw "Antonia or anybody took the "alleged fifty pieces one peso coin with Tamaraw Emblem"; Therefore, there was doubt as to the fact that "accused Antonia 'took' the fifty pieces of one peso coin with Tamaraw Emblem";

(2) That even the "alleged" fact that "fifty pieces of one peso coin with Tamaraw Emblem" was placed by complainant on top of her dresser cabinet when she took a bath was not proven and was just a "say so" or merely alleged, by the complainant; We do not even know whether complainant really took a bath or not";,
There was laughter in the courtroom.

(3) That no one was certain that as a matter fact there were fifty pieces of one peso coin with Tamaraw Emblem belonging to the complainant that were in fact lost;

(4) That the pieces of one peso coin with Tamaraw Emblem was found inside the "Talcum Baby Powder plastic container owned by accused Antonia Dela Cruz inside her "Tampipi" inside her room, give rise to a legal presumption that the 'talcum baby powder plastic container' and its contents, belong to accused Antonia,;

(5) That the 'talcum baby powder plastic container ' was found inside the 'tampipi' owned by accused Antonia, in her room, legally presumed that the tampipi and everything in it was owned by Antonia, there being no contrary evidence, please remember, "no one saw Antonia took the fifty pieces of one peso coin with 'Tamaraw Emblem".

(6) That the police found fifty pieces of one peso coin with 'Tamaraw Emblem' in the 'talcum baby powder plastic container' owned by accused Antonia does not prove that the fifty pieces of one peso coin with 'tamaraw emblem' were the same fifty pieces of one peso coin "allegedly "owned by the complainant as was definitely shown during the "cross examination" that not even one piece of the said coin bear any name, or mark or sign as to identify as to who it belongs to; The legal presumption even lean in favor of accused Antonia that "Antonia owns the pieces of one peso coin found in the plastic container, in her 'tampipi' in her room.

(7) That Antonia was allegedly paid Thirty Pesos in one peso coin with tamaraw emblem every month for 11 months strongly indicate that Antonia can and may 'save' fifty pesos in one peso coin and even more, considering that Antonia did not go out of the house for 11 months and has no way to spend her wages.

(8) That Antonia had no visitor for 11 months strongly indicate that

she had no way to give away her wages to other people, hence may even save more than fifty pesos of her wages.

(9) That as the complainant had not proven any one single coin as hers, her claim that the coins inside the container of the Talcum baby powder plastic container was hers necessarily must fail too;

(10) That as the accused has in her favor the Constitutional right to be presumed "innocent" until proven otherwise by proof beyond resonable doubt, then necessarily she should be declared innocent of the charge, by legal presumption, and the case against her dismissed.

Wherefore, we respectfully reiterate our fervent prayer to Dismiss the case against the accused. Thank You Your Honor.

Court: In view of the "King Solomon Like" demonstration by defense counsel, showing the merit of the accused prayer for "dismissal" of the case against her to be meritorious the prayer of accused through counsel to dismiss the case against her is hereby "Granted" the case is therefore "Dismissed" without cost and the released of the accused is hereby ordered "Immediately" unless she is being held for some other legal impediments.

"So Ordered."

The accused leaped for joy.

Mr. And Mrs. Teng looked at me in disbelief.

Mr. Teng whispered to me, I know the accused will win her case, but I did not expect to be this soon. Thank you Attorney Santiago.

I smiled and looked above as I said my fervent prayer, "Thank you Lord God Almighty. Praise be Your Name Forever. Amen."

Chapter VII

Mr. Teng And The ASSO
That Did Not Bite

(Names* fictional/events factual)

Mr. Teng and I became client-friends and soon became buddy-buddy. His wife trusted me so that Mr. Teng had to call me by phone at nights whenever he would like to go gallivanting so that I will accompany him and be his "pass".

I was asked by Mr. Teng to handle the cases of his company per case and pay me per piecework.

One day I came from Calamba, Laguna and went straight to the VIP Coffee Shop at VIP Building, at Dewey Boulevard, our usual meeting place of Mr. Teng, the President and owner of the Insurance company, to report to Mr. Teng my findings on the "double payment" of an insured passenger paid by the Regional Branch Officer of the Company. Mr. Teng was not at the coffee shop so I proceeded to his office at the Insurance company at the fourth floor of the building. His Insurance Branch Office occupies the fourth floor.

When I entered the Insurance, I sensed something was wrong. Usually when I enter the Insurance office, the receptionist, the typist and other employees were busy typing, sorting papers, walking to and fro and they greet me with smile and "hello "since they know their boss and I were buddy-buddy -- but that day was different. The people in the office were dreadfully silent. So I asked what could be wrong. I was then told that Mr. Teng and his whole family, his son Eduard, daughters Roseanne, and Donna, and his grandchildren aged 3 and 4 were at their house and were being held by soldiers and will be brought to Camp Crame for "Large Scale Estafa (Swindling), for Violation of Bouncing Checks Law worth One Million Pesos" and more. I told them I will go at once to the house of Mr. Teng to find out what really happened.

Martial Law was in effect throughout the Philippines as declared by then President Marcos. People brought to Camp Crame were good as dead, no visitors allowed, mobility restricted and stories of tortures, physical as well as psychological, were told around so mere mention of the camp bring shiver to the bone.

It was one of those days that Mr. Teng and his family, his son Eduard, daughters Roseanne and Donna and grandchildren aged 3 and 4 were being held in their house by soldiers and threatened to be brought to Camp Crame.

I hurriedly drove my Hillman "Hunter Car" the car paid to me by Col. Magnalonso II as my acceptance fee. and went to the house of Mr. Teng., as fast as I could. The house of Mr. Teng was in a compound with concrete fence and iron gate in "Amang Rodriguez Avenue, Quezon City. From afar I saw two army trucks with capacity of 60 soldiers. I saw some of the soldiers surrounding the outside perimeter of the house, while some of the soldiers stood in front of the gate so that no one may come in or go out without passing them.

I parked my car in front of the gate and got off the car. I was then in brown coat and tie of white, blue and red combination and brown shoes,.I was slim. 5'5 tall, and Pilipino colored brown-- some say I look like Marcos, the President.

I said hello to the soldiers and said:

Santiago: Hello there soldier, I am Atty. Santiago. My clients own the house inside. Why are there soldiers surrounding the house.?

As I addressed this remarks in "English" to the soldiers guarding the outside gate, the soldiers motioned me to go ahead and approach the iron door of the concrete gate. I approached the iron door of the concrete gate and knocked at the iron door.

After a while, a soldier peeped outside the gate from the inside, eyed me thoroughly,. But before he could speak I spoke first and said in "English":

Atty. Santiago: I am Atty. Santiago, the owner of the house inside are my clients, why are there soldiers outside and inside the house? I want to talk to the highest ranking officer..

The soldier I was talking to pulled his head inside and called in Tagalog vernacular, saying "somebody is here, looked like President Marcos, he want to talk to Sir –

Another soldier peeped outside the iron door, eyed me, then said in a loud voice in Tagalog vernacular "Call Sir, somebody in "Americana" (meaning, in coat and tie) is here, he want to talk to Sir".

Then somebody inside in an officer's suite, ordered the soldiers to open the door and let that "Atty. Santiago" to come in..

The soldiers opened the door and motioned me to come in.

I told myself, "shall I come in?," "What if after I come in these soldiers will not allow me to go out anymore?"

I answered myself, "of course. As a friend and lawyer of Mr. Teng and his family, you must come in and see that their Constitutional rights are respected and protect them from abuse, and oppression, so "bahala na", meaning, ' God to take care of the rest.'

So, I went inside, while saying aloud:

Atty. Santiago: I am atty. Santiago. The owner of the house and his family are my clients. I want to talk to them.

A soldier in an officer's uniform approached me and said:

Lieutenant Salve: I am Lieutenant Salve. The soldiers here are under my command, Why are you here, Atty. Santiago.?

Atty. Santiago: Mr. Lieutenant, I was told Mr. Teng and his family, his son and daughters and grandchildren were being held by soldiers inside their house, I came here as their lawyer. As you know, The President, Mr. Marcos is a lawyer. He was topnotcher during his time when he took the Bar Examination. So even though he has declared Martial Law in the Philippines, he respect the law and surely will not allow his soldiers to be disrespectful to the law. Now, tell me Mr Lieutenant, by what authority of law, did you come here? What crime did my clients do?, Why are there soldiers surrounding the house.? Why are there soldiers in the house.? Do you have any Warrant of Arrest, Mr. Lieutenant?

I bombarded the Lieutenant with legal questions.

Lieutenant Salve: We are only assisting the NBI to enforce ASSO (Arrest, Search and Seizure Order).

Atty. Santiago: Oh is that so? Then I would like to see the ASSO for verification as to its due execution. Where is that ASSO Mr. Lieutenant?

Lieutenant Salve: It was with the NBI Team Leader, I was told. I will call him so you may talk to him yourself, Atty. Santiago.

Atty. Santiago: Alright I will talk to my clients while you are are calling him,. Thank you. Where are my clients Mr. Lieutenant?

Lieutenant Salve: In the house, Atty. Santiago.

I went inside the house at once and saw Mr. Teng, his wife Dona Margarita, his son Eduard, and his daughters Roseanne and Donna, and her children, a girl 3 years old and son 4 years old.

I approached Mr. Teng, and greeted him,

Atty Santiago: How are you Sir? What is this about. Why are there soldiers surrounding your house?

Mr. Teng, his face haggard and apprehensive, answered me:

Mr. Teng: We have just taken our breakfast when the soldiers led by Lieutenant Salve came to the house and told us that they were assisting the NBI team led by one Atty. Sanchez and accused me and all other officers of the Insurance Company I own, of violation of "Large Scale Estafa - Bouncing Checks of One Million Pesos and above" and told me that the said charge is unbailable, without bail, and that by the law on ASSO, that is, law on arrest, search and seizure order, directive of the Department of National Defense, he will haul us all to Camp Crame. So, I told Atty. Sanchez, I do not want my family and I to be hauled to Camp Crame as it will be damaging to our reputation as businessman and will have adverse effect on our Insurance Company and will also be a traumatic experience to my wife and daughers and my grandchildren, and asked him, is there anything we can do to fix this problem?

Atty. Santiago: What did Atty Sanchez reply, Sir?

Mr. Teng: Atty. Sanchez then told me that my statement I just made was "Attempted bribery of an officer of the law, and he laughed.. and told me what I want to do may be accomplished without much "hush-hush" by a lawyer working for me like my golf-playmate, Atty Francis who was then in the office of the Insurance Company when the NBI team he was heading came to enforce the ASSO and volunteered to accompany them here. After talking to the NBI team leader, Atty. Francis approached me and told me he can be the bridge, if I want, for a smooth "cashunduan" and silent "money obra "with the NBI team so that the NBI will no longer pursue the charge of Large Scale Estafa - of Bouncing Check of One Million Pesos and more".

Atty. Santiago: So what did you say, Sir?, I asked Mr. Teng.

Mr. Teng: I was then hoping you would come to the house by chance and get us out of this tight situation, although I knew you would go to Calamba, as I told you to investigate the Calamba "double payment" paid by the Regional Branch Manager of the Company to a passenger insured by the Company. However, as I do not want my family and I to be hauled to Camp Crame and suffer more of this dreadful traumatic experience I told Atty. Francis to go ahead and I will prepare the One Million Pesos Cash. I called the office at San Fernando Pampanga where the husband of Donna was assigned Treasurer of the Company to send over to Manila Office One Million Pesos Cash by 3 o'clock in the afternoon, today, so that Atty. Sanchez will not bring the ASSO here anymore and the NBI will leave us, already --

That's the "cashunduan "Mr. Teng confided to me..

Atty. Santiago: You were pressured Sir. Anyway you did it all for your family. But if I had come here earlier then I could have prevented your suffering. Still I will see what I can do to get you out of this miserable situation --

At that point of our conversation, the NBI team leader Atty. Sanchez entered the sala of the house where we were talking and took a chair near us and asked me:

Atty. Sanchez: Atty. Santiago, I was told by Lieutenant Salve you want to talk to me,?

Atty. Santiago: Ah, yes Atty. Sanchez, I am the lawyer of Mr. Teng and his family, I came here to report to Mr. Teng my findings about the double payment paid by the company regional manager of a region, and I was surprised to see so many soldiers surrounding the house of Mr. Teng - so I asked the Lieutenant by what authority of law his soldiers are surrounding the house; he told me his soldiers were assisting the NBI enforce the ASSO; so I asked the Lieutenant where was the ASSO, it was then that Lieutenant Salve told me it is better that I ask you myself;

Atty. Sanchez: Yes, you ask me now, Panero.

Atty. Santiago: Yes, Where is the ASSO, Atty. Sanchez?

Atty. Sanchez: ASSO, that's Arrest, Search and Seizure Order, a directive of the Department of National Defense, your clients are being charged with Large Scale Estafa with Bouncing Checks of One Million Pesos and more. That's unbailable, as you know. Also no warrant of arrest required, and once arrested, they will be hauled and held at Camp Crame –

And Atty Sanchez paused to give time for Mr. Teng to realize how serious the situation he was in.

I looked at Mr. Teng. His face became pale and nervous..

I thought to myself, this is a battle of wit, he was using psychology to attain an illegal purpose.. a Million Pesos "cashunduan".

Atty. Santiago: So where is the ASSO, Mr. NBI team leader, You will agree with me Atty. Sanchez it is the right of my clients to see that ASSO, and determine its due execution, is it not?

Atty. Sanchez: Ahh, -- the ASSO is with the NBI main at Taft Avenue. Panero.

Atty. Santiago: So, it was not with you,? You have no ASSO to show, then you have no ASSO to enforce, right, Panero?

Mr. Teng smiled and said,:

Mr. Teng: I forgot to ask Atty. Sanchez, about that ASSO.

Mr. Teng whispered to me, "Atty Santiago you are really razor-sharp.

I thought to myself, I must have the sympathy of the soldiers. so I said:

Atty. Santiago: As it is already noontime, time to eat lunch, I wil order for all of us pansit and bread, coffee and soft drinks from the pansiteria nearby. Ok?

Mr. Teng: Okay, I will call our suki, Pansiteria to deliver pansit, bread, coffee and soft drinks, for all of us and the soldiers too.

The soldiers smiled and whispered to each other, "at least we will have lunch".

Atty. Sanchez: I will call the main NBI office at Taft Avenue to send the ASSO here, Atty. Santiago Then we will haul your clients to Camp Crame.

I thought to myself, this Atty. Sanchez is pursuing his threat, I looked at Mr. Teng, he was nervous again. His wife Margarita, daughters Roseanne and Donna looked at each other, their eyes expressing extreme apprehension –

I asked Atty. Sanchez --

Atty. Santiago: Where are the complainants against Mr. Teng, Atty. Sanchez, if I may ask?

Atty. Sanchez: They are at NBI Main executing their affidavit-complaints, answered the NBI team leader.

Atty. Santiago: Eh, is that so, how many complainants were they,?

Atty. Sanchez: Well, many, about ten or twenty, maybe.

Atty. Santiago: So, it is now three (3 o'clock) P.M., Mr. Teng what time did you tell the Treasurer from Pampanga to bring the cash here?

Mr. Teng: I told the Treasurer, husband of Donna, to bring the Cash here before 3 o'clock P.M., today.

Atty. Sanchez retorted:

Atty. Sanchez: If my men come back from the NBI main office with the ASSO before that treasurer arrives, I will enforce the ASSO and haul your clients to Camp Crame, Atty. Santiago.

Another repetition of the threat, I told myself. I know Atty, Sanchez was bluffing as he has no ASSO and there will be no ASSO to come since the elements of Large Scale Estafa (Swindling) by Bouncing Checks are not complete, so I will just call his bluff --

I asked Mr. Teng:

Atty. Santiago: Did you or your Insurance issue a check for One Million (Php 1,000,000) Pesos to anyone of the ten or twenty complainants in this alleged Large scale Estafa by Bouncing Check, Mr. Teng?

Mr. Teng: No. I have not issued any check for One Million Pesos (Php 1.000,000) to anyone of the ten or twenty complainants.

Atty Santiago: Who are these complainants, What are their names, Atty. Sanchez?, I asked Atty. Sanchez.

Atty. Sanchez: Here are the records of the names and adresses and amount of the checks issued to them, and xerox copies of the checks. Add all the checks and they will amount to One Million (Php 1 Million) Pesos.

Atty. Santiago: When did you file the Complaint for Large Scale Estafa by Bouncing Checks, Atty. Sanchez?

Atty. Sanchez perspired tremendously as if in the hot seat of the interrogation room.

Atty. Sanchez: Soon we have the Affidavit Complaint of the complainants, I will file it in court of Manila City, Atty. Santiago.

I looked at the faces of Mr. Teng and the faces of his wife and children to see their reaction -- but maybe they were all terrified of the threat that they had not noticed the meaning of my quetions and the legal implications of the answer to my questions by Atty. Sanchez.

Then I called the Lieutenant:

Atty. Santiago: Mr. Lieutenant Salve, I understand you are only doing your duty, as you were requested by Atty. Sanchez to assist him in enforcing the ASSO. You thought all the while you are performing a bounden duty as an officer and a gentleman --Right?

Lieutenant Salve: Right, Atty. Santiago. I was requested by Atty. Sanchez of the NBI to assist him in enforcing the ASSO, so my soldiers and I were here since 9 AM this day, to see to it that the ASSO was enforced.

Atty. Sanchez: That"s correct Atty. Santiago, what is your point.?

Atty. Santiago: My point is clear, Gentlemen, Mr. Lieutenant Salve was rendering a legal service in assisting you, Atty. Sanchez in enforcing the ASSO, for that he should be commended, however, you Atty. Sanches had no ASSO in your possession, and I am sure, you would not be able to obtain an ASSO even up to 5 PM since the elements of the alleged crime of "Large Scale Estafa (Swindling) by Bouncing Checks of One Million Pesos and more "were not present and therefore, no ASSO will be issued by the proper authorities of the Department of National Defense.

At this point Mr. Teng, his wife Dona Margarita, his son Eduard, his daughters Roseanne and Donna were all looking at me intently and in suspense, -- then I continued:

Atty. Santiago: So, since there was no ASSO from the beginning, since 9 AM in the morning of this day up to now, 4:30 in the afternoon, almost 7 hours and thirty minutes, Mr. Teng and his family, his wife Dona Margarita, his son Eduard, his daughters Roseanne, and Donna, have been restricted in their movements, and were actually "arrested", by Atty. Sanchez, and by Mr. Lieutenant Salve, "Illegally" and with no authority since there was no ASSO to talk about, then Atty. Sanchez and Mr. Lieutenant Salve will be prosecuted in accordance with law for "Coercion "and/or "Illegal Detention" and "Illegal Extortion".

Mr. Teng, his wife Dona Margarita, his son Eduard, his daughters Roseanne and Donna, were now smiling and clapped their hands.

The soldiers then were around us gathered by the clapping of hands.

Atty. Santiago: Even the Department of National Defense and the Armed Forces of the Philippines will question the "whereabout "of the 60 soldiers, under the command of Lieutenant Salve who have gone "awol" (absence without leave) assisting an "illegal" operation.

The Lieutenant abruptly stood up and pointed his finger in accusing manner to Atty. Sanchez, as he said "Pahamak ka Atty. Sanchez, all the while I thought I was performing a legal duty in providing you assistance to enforce ASSO but instead you have been using me to do an illegal act, as he called his soldiers in a commanding manner --:

Lieutenant Salve: "Soldiers, disarm Atty. Sanchez and the NBI team," then he turned to me and, said, "Atty. Santiago, I am sorry this happened, I was wrong in not asking Atty. Sanchez to show me the ASSO which I thought he had in his possession. He nearly destroyed my career as an officer".

Atty. Santiago: Alright Mr. Lieutenant Salve, what do you intend to do now?

Lieutenant Salve: We will return to barracks and turn over Atty. Sanchez and his men to our superior officer at Camp Crame for using the Armed Forces Of the Phlippines in an "Illegal Operation".

Then Lieutenant Salve turned to me and smiled, and said:

Lieutenant Salve: Thank you Atty. Santiago for enlightening me otherwise, I could have been party to an illegal act and my career destroyed.

Then Lieutenant Salve turned to Mr. Teng and his family and said:

Lieutenant Salve: "My soldiers and I apologize for the inconvenience brought about by this incident."

Mr. Teng, his wife and children heaved a sigh of relief.

Then Lieutenant Salve ordered his soldiers to "Go back to Barracks" and took Atty. Sanchez and the NBI team to Camp Crame.

Mr. Teng: Atty Santiago, the Lieutenant arrested Atty. Sanchez and said he will bring him and the NBI team to Camp Crame..

Atty. Santiago: That was his way out to avoid being discharged from the Armed Forces, imagine he used the soldiers in an illegal operation because of "ignorance" not fit for an officer.

Mr. Teng: You are so brave, and witty Atty. Santiago. I and my family thank you for getting us out of such a tight situation. Even without us asking for your help, you rendered us your professional legal service, so it is just and proper that we compensate you for that, -- then Mr. Teng pulled out his wallet and handed me all its contents, then he said softly but audible enough to be heard by his Mrs. and children, "we thank you Atty. Santiago."

Donna Margarita, the wife of Mr. Teng whispered to me,:

Donna Margarita: Thank you Atty. Santiago for saving us from this horrible experience, while we cannot thank you enough by words, maybe this will somehow compensate your legal effort, as she handed to me a bunch of paper money bills she took from her pant's back pocket.

Atty. Francis did not come back to the house of Mr. Teng., by 5 o'clock. He did not play golf with Mr, Teng eversince.

When I went to the rest room and counted the money Mr. Teng gave me, it was Thirteen Thousand (Php 13,000) Pesos all in One Thousand Peso bills. A lucky number. While the bunch of paper bills Donna Margarita gave me was Seven Thousand (Php 7,000) Pesos, so all in all the Teng gave me a total of Twenty Thousand (Php 20,000) Pesos. Good enough for a day's work, anyway I saved them a Million Pesos from an attempted "illegal extortion".

I looked up and murmured fervently, "Thank You Lord God Almighty. Praise be Thy name. Forever" Amen.

Chapter VIII

Give Me Liberty Or Give Me Death —The Ms. Luz Valdezrama 2.8 Million Pesos Estafa (Swindling) Case

(names* fictional/ events factual)

One fine afternoon while I was sipping coffee at the Vip Building Coffee Shop at Dewey Boulevard, Manila, Mr. Teng, my client-friend, the President-owner of a big inurance company issuing bailbonds, bonds, motor vehicle insurance, fire, and other insurance papers, approached me and introduced his companion, a fine looking, beautiful woman about 35 years of age, fair complexion, and said to me:

Mr. Teng: Attorney Santiago, this is Ms. Luz Valdezrama, a long-time friend of the family. She is requesting me to issue her a 2.8 Million Peso bailbond. She was charged of Estafa of 2.8 Million Pesos pending with the Fiscal's office of Rizal at Kapitolyo, Pasig, Rizal, with initial hearing tomorrow at 2 o'clock. I told her "okay" with me but since she has no "collateral ""for such amount of bailbond I want to make sure she has a fighting chance of acquittal so I need to know her lawyer. She told me she has no lawyer up to now, so -- will you look into her case Atty, Santiago and tell me if I can take the risk of 2.8 Million Pesos bailbond without collatral?

Atty Santiago: Well, an accused "who has a fighting lawyer, who has a winning case, will surely not abscond, that is, will not run away from the charge -- that will defend on her lawyer - -make her lawyer, her guarantor, Sir.

I address Mr. Teng with "Sir" because I respect him as a father, and he like me like a son, but he knew I am professional with my dealings with him, that I tell him white is white and black is black, inspite of our personal mutual respect and friendship.

Mr. Teng: Alright, Ms Luz Valdezrama. Tell him your case.

Ms Luz Valdezrama, began her story:

Luz Valdezrama: Well. Atty. Santiago, I am working as a "real estate agent" for those who want to buy or sell real estate. One day, I was approached by a lady-friend agent, Ms. Co and she told me that her client-friend would like to buy a lot worth 2.8 Million Pesos in the vicinity of Shaw Boulevard and Wack-Wack Golf Club in Mandaluyong, Rizal; that her buyer will give us 3% of 2.8 agent's fee which we will divide half-half; so each of us two will have Php 42,000.00 pesos each.

I told my friend I will look for her "order" at once.

By some good luck, another agent-friend of mine, Ms Dory Go, told me that her client-friend was selling her lot Titled TCT No. 123456 situated in a compound, enclosed by concrete wall in Shaw Boulevard, near Wack-Wack Golf Club, Mandaluyong, Rizal for Php 2.5 M and will give "selling commission "of 3% of Php 2.5 which we will divide between us two.

I told myself "What a luck" just what I am looking for. So I immdiately contacted my friend, Dory Go, and told her that I have already found a buyer for the property she was selling, but so as to protect our agent's seller commission of 3% of php 2.5 I will give the owner of the lot Php 300,000 as binding agreement just give us time to complete the payment of balance of Php 2.2 M within 30 days If I fail to complete the payment then she (the lot seller) can forfeit in her favor my Php 300,000 as damages and penalty, I want this put in writing in black and white. My friend Dory Go told me she will arrange the agreement at once, "just be ready with your money, Luz" said Dory Go.

Sometime later, Dory Go told me the agreement I want was already ready for signing.

So I at once contacted my friend Ms Sally Co to arrange an appointment with her buyer-client to formalize things as I have already found the lot she want to buy. Thus we went to the house of the buyer at Shaw Boulevard about a few blocks from the lot I was selling. Sally Co introduced to me the buyer as Mrs Chona Sy, a Filipina married to a Chinese meztizo doing business in America.

I described to Mrs. Chona Sy the lot I was selling for Php. 2.8 Million Pesos with Title No. 123456 containing an area of One Thousand Four Hundred (1,400 Sq. M.) Square Meters, more or less; The lot is in a compound enclosed with concrete wall along Shaw Blvd. near Wack –Wack Golf Club, Mandaluyong, Rizal.

Mrs Chona Sy told me she was glad I found already the lot she want to buy and asked me when she and the lot owner can talk to formalize the deal, I told Mrs Sy that as I have found the lot I am entitled to 3% of Php 2.8 M buyer-commission to which Mrs Sy, agreed.

I opened to her that I am also the seller, to which Mrs Sy said that it's okay to her, she will still buy the lot and told me she will call her lawyer to prepare the "Deed of Assignment" so we can sign it tomorrow and then she will pay me the whole purchase price of Php 2.8 M Pesos.

I told Mrs Sy that while she told me that she was already willing to buy the lot and even told me she will call her lawyer to prepare the "Deed of Assignment" I told Mrs Sy that there were other people in the past that told me they will buy the lot, that it's a "done deal, we will buy the lot" but back out at the last moment, so if Mrs Sy was really sincere in buying the lot then she will give me now the 3% buyer-commission and a binding partial payment of Php 500,000.00 so by tomorrow when we sign the "Deed of Assignment" then she can complete the payment by paying the balance of Php 2.3 M pesos.

Mrs Sy then said that's okay, no problem. Then she stood up and took from a cabinet a bundle of money and counted Php 82,000.00 pesos and handed it to me saying, "Luz here is Php 82,000 for you as agent's buyer-commission and she again counted Php 500,000. Pesos and said, Ms Luz, here is Php 500,000. Pesos for partial payment for the lot. I am not like other people you talked to, when I say "Done, I will buy it" it's done, I do not back out.

"Just give me a receipt for the partial payment -- even in your hand-writing,, I am not very formal as to receipts, never mind the Php 82,000 Pesos, even without receipt, that's small to bother us, okay?" Added Mrs. Sy.

While I was writing the receipt for the Php 500,000, Pesos partial payme nt of Mrs. Chona Sy, she continued, "tomorrow morning when my lawyer arrived with the "Deed of Assignment" I will call you Ms Luz, so that you can come over and we can both sign the "Deed of Assignment" then I will pay you the whole purchase price, Okay? Then Mrs Sy called her lawyer and told the lawyer to prepare the "deed of Assignment" at once and bring it to her house tomorrow morning as soon as possible, for our signature. I then thank Mrs Sy and I went out of the house.

As I went out of the house of Mrs. Sy, I felt a little embarrassed at the look of Mrs. Sy gave me as if saying to me that I did not trust her, while she trusted me.

Atty. Santiago: So what happened next, if any, Ms Luz Valdezrama?

Ms. Luz Valdzrama looked at me with sad, apprehensive eyes. as she continued:

Ms. Luz Valdezrama: As far as I remembered, my receipt, In my handwriting was as follows:

"Receipt   September 20 2000

"RECEIVED FROM MRS CHONA SY The sum of Five Hundred Thousand (Php500,000.00) Pesos as partial payment for the Lot with TCT no. 123456 1,400 Square Meters more or less situated in a compound enclosed with concrete fence along Shaw Boulevard near Wack –Wack Golf Club, Mandaluyong, Rizal. Balance of Two Million Three Hundred Thousand (Php 2,300,000) Pesos as full payment of purchase price payable on or before 12th day from signing of Deed of Assignment. Failure of Assignee / buyer to complete full payment of purchase price on or before the 12th day from the signing of the Deed of Assignment the Five Hundred Thousand (Php 500,000) Pesos partial payment shall be forfeited in favor of the Assignor/ Seller as penalty and damages.

"Done in Mandaluyong, Rizal this 20th day of September 2000". "(SGD) LUZ VALDEZRAMA Assignor/Seller"

Ms Luz Valdezrama paused to catch her breath after which she continued --

Ms. Luz Valdezrama: I told myself, I must give myself a blowout for having made a good transaction. So after I have deposited the money in my bank I went to the movie and ate dinner in a class restaurant.

The money was not mine alone, I will give half of Php 84,000 to Sally Co, half of Php 75,000 to Dory Go and the Php 300,000 to the owner of the lot as binding partial payment so that after Mrs Chona Sy pay the full price of Php 2,300,000 I can pay the lot owner Php 2,200,000 so I will have for myself Php 37,500 plus Php 42,000 plus Php 100,000 summa total I will have for myself Php 379,500.

That's how real estate agents earn in buying/selling for clients continued Ms Luz Valdezrama.

When I came home that night, I was surprised to see Mrs Chona Sy waiting for me outside my apartment I was renting. She told me her husband doing business in America called her by phone after I had gone home. Her husband told her that he want to show his business associates that they (Mr and Mrs Sy) had real estate properties near Wack-Wack Golf Club known to his associates as prime lots, so that when Mrs. Sy told her husband that Mrs Sy and I had concluded our Deed of Assignment and that the lawyer of Mrs Sy will bring the papers for signing tomorow morning, Mr Sy asked her to immediately fax to him even a "bogus Deed of Assignment" (nightime in Philippines daytime in America) so as to show it at once to his associates so they will recognize him as their leader in their group, so Mrs Sy rushed to me to ask me to sign the bogus deed of assignment Mrs Sy made herself. So just to help Mrs Sy and as I said to myself, anyway the real Deed of Assignment will be ready by tomorow morning, a few hours from that moment, so what harm will it do. So, Ms Luz said, "I signed the bogus Deed of Assignment"

Ms Luz continued, Mrs Sy told me: "Do not worry Ms. Luz, in a few hours from now, it will be morning, my lawyer will bring the real Deed of Assignment, and as soon as my lawyer arrive at my house, I will call you Ms Luz so you can come over and we will sign it togther, then I will pay you," continued Ms Luz.

Atty Santiago: So you signed the "Bogus Deed of Assignment", Ms Luz?, I asked her.

Ms. Luz continued: As soon as I had handed to Mrs. Sy the Bogus Deed of Assignment. Mrs Sy went home" --

Early morning the next day I prepared myself, dress up and waited for the call of Mrs Sy. However Mrs Sy did not call the whole day. The next day, Mrs Sy did not call either, and the next day, still no call.

I told myself, Mrs Sy must be very busy --

The next day, I called the house of Mrs Sy., no response.

I thought to myself, Mrs Sy must have gone to America --moneyed people do that, they were here now, the next hour they were in America, they have ready visa to go anywhere they like..

One night I was surprised to hear the voice of Mrs Chona Sy calling me from America and told me that she suffered an adverse business setback so she was recooping all money from all sources so as to recover from a financial fall so she was requesting me to return her Php 500,000 Peso partial payment which will help her a lot she told me. I answered her that the money she gave me has already been forfeited as damages and penalty according to our agreement, however, I told her I will try to give her Php 200,000 Pesos out of my own pocket to help her. She insisted on her demand that I return the whole Php 500,000 Pesos so I gave her my final answer "No way";

Then some weeks after, I myself had become busy with new clients that time passed by swiftly, almost unnoticed.

One day I was shocked to receive a letter of demand from the lawyer of Mrs Sy demanding that I return to Mrs Chona Sy at their office within 15 days from my receipt of the letter Two Million Eight Hundred Thousand (Php 2,800.000) Pesos paid to me by Chona Sy, his client, for me to Cede, Transfer and Convey Lot TCT No. 123456 described and mentioned in the attached "Deed of Assignment", marked annex "A": Failure on my part to heed his demand will cause him to file Estafa case against me which will destroy my image and reputation and may cause my imprisonment for at least twenty (20) years.

A photocopy of the "Bogus "Deed of Assignment" was attached, as follows:

"DEED OF ASSIGNMENT"

I Luz Valdezrama of legal age, Filipino, Single, residing at Las Vegas Street, Mandaluyong, Rizal, for and in consideration of the sum of TWO MILLION EIGHT HUNDRED THOUSAND (Php 2,800,000) PESOS receipt of which is hereby acknowledged from Mrs Chona Sy of legal age, Filipino, married to James Sy, Filipino, of legal age, residing at Nevada Street, Mandaluyong, Rizal, do hereby Cede, Transfer and Convey to Mrs Chona Sy by way of Deed of Assignment (description of lot omitted) the hereinbelow particularly described Lot with TCT No. 123456 with area of One Thousand Four Hundred (1,400 Sq. M.) Square Meters, more or less. enclosed by concrete wall situated along Shaw Boulevard, Mandaluyong, Rizal., near the Wack –Wack Golf Club, which lot I, Luz Valdezrama, am the lawful and legitimate owner.

Witness my hand this 20th day of September 2000 at Mandaluyong, Rizal.

Sgd Luz Valdezrama
Assignor/Seller

REPUBLIC OF THE PHILIPPINES)–
MANDALUYONG, R I Z A L)

Before me. Notary Public for Mandaluyong, Rizal, this 20th day of September 2000 appeared Ms Luz Valdezrama with Non-Professional Driver's License 234567890 issued by the Land Transportation Office Manila East Agency to expire December 2000 and she acknowledged to me that the foregoing Deed of Assignment is her own, true, free and voluntary act and deed.

Witness my hand and seal this 20th day of September 2000 at Mandaluyong, Rizal.

SGD ILLEGIBLE

NOTARY PUBLIC My Commission Expires
DECEMBER 31 2001

Doc 123 Page 23

Book II Ser. 2000

Then Ms Luz Valdezrama continued:

Ms Luz Valdezrama: "To tell you the truth, Atty Santiago, I almost collapsed. I thought I was going to have a heart attack or a stroke. Where would I get that Php 2,800,000 Pesos. Mrs Chona Sy just gave me Php 84,00 0 for agent's -buyer commission, Php 500,000 Pesos for partial payment of the lot, I gave half of the Agent's -Buyer commission to Sally Co. half of agent's commission for agent-seller commission to Dory Go, and Php 300,000 to the owner of the lot to bind her to me for thirty (30) days to sell to me her lot so that I may sell it to Mrs Chona Sy within 12 days time so summa total out of the transaction I earned Php 279,000 Pesos, only. So where will I get that money, Atty Santiago? -- Is that just and fair?

Atty. Santiago: Of Course that's not fair. That will amount to "Unjust Enrichment" in favor of Mrs Sy, but how could I tell, I was not there, how could I tell who is telling the truth, You or Mrs Sy?

Ms Luz Valdezrama: I don't want to go to prison, Atty Santiago, I would rather commit suicide than go to prison – Give me liberty or give me death -- help me, Atty. Santiago.

I looked at her. She was crying. I took pity on her, so I told her:

Atty Santiago: Of Course I will help you I will not let you be imprisoned just for alleged Php 500,000, Pesos but promise me you will not commit suicide, Okay Ms Luz?,

Ms Luz Valdezrama "Okay I will not commit suicide Attorney.

Atty Santiago: Alright, What do you want me to do for you, Ms. Luz Valdezrama?

Ms Luz Valdezrama: I want you to be my lawyer, Atty. Santiago. –
Atty. Santiago: But why me, you don't know me –

Ms Luz Valdezrama: I know Mr Teng. His wife was Miss Manila, my mother's best friend. Mr. Teng is a good businessman.

He has a way to judge people. I noted he was willing to give me bailbond even without collateral at your "say so ", that meanss he trust you so much as to take a risk worth Php 2,800,000 Pesos. If he can trust you with that much money surely I can also.

Atty Santiago: By the way, may I call you Luz short for Ms Luz

Valdezrama??

Ms Luz Valdezrama - Of course, Atty. Santiago

Atty Santiago: Of course you will understand I charge my clients, acceptance fees - 20% of the amount involved in the case, plus appearance fees Php 2,000 every time I appear in court postponed or not, plus attorney's fees 25% of the amount received by my client from the adverse party by decision or amicable settlement.

Ms Luz Valdezrama: So how much will I pay you Atty Santiago?

Atty Santiago: By the way, Luz, do you have a duplicate of the

receipt you gave Mrs Chona Sy? I asked her;

Ms Luz Valdezrama: None. Atty Santiago.

Atty Santiago: What about the "bogus" Deed of Assignment", do you have a duplicate? I asked Luz again.

Luz answered: None, also, Atty Santiago

Atty Santiago: So it appears that you have a hard case to defend, Luz -- first, Mrs Chona Sy holds a "Deed of Assignment" duly notarized, Second, You have no document to show that you ceded, transferred and conveyed to Chona Sy the lot -- that's clear estafa (swindling).

Ms Luz (short for Luz Valdezrama): So, what shall I do, then?

Atty Santiago "Then you will have to fight a hard court battle --Get a sharp, fighting lawyer..

Ms Luz: That's it, Atty Santiago, I want you to fight the case for me. -- Just tell me, how much I will pay your profeessional fee?

Atty. Santiago: Alright, as both of us want to be professional about this case, just pay me Php 50,000.00 - no more appearance fees; BUT --

Ms Luz: Okay, I will give the acceptance fees, today - and what do you mean by that "BUT" Atty Santiago,? asked Ms Luz as she smiled at me sheepishly.

I looked at her and laughed, and told Ms Luz, I was not that naughty --what I meant was that "you Ms Luz" must help me by praying hard, real hard, so we will win your case -- I don't want to lose any case.

Ms Luz: Ahhh. Well, I am sorry for what I thought you meant, Atty. Santiago. I will pray real hard that we win my case; Thank you for not charging me appearance fees anymore.

Atty Santiago: Alright Ms Luz, now you can tell Mr. Teng, I had agreed to handle your case so he may issue the bailbond..

Ms Luz Valdezrama: I will go now, Atty. Santiago, but I will be back, to give your acceptance fee..

I ordered another coffee while Ms Luz went upstairs to the office of Mr. Teng for the bailbond..

Soon Ms. Luz and Mr. Teng walked into the coffee shop.

Mr. Teng: Ms Luz told me you agreed to handle her case, was that right, Atty. Santiago?

Atty Santiago: Correct, Sir.

Mr. Teng: The hearing at the fiscal's office will be tomorrow, 2 o'clock at Kapitolyo, Pasig. Do you need the bailbond now? Asked Mr. Teng.

Atty. Santiago: I think the fiscal will find "Probable Cause" so he will file the case against the respondent, Ms. Luz Valdezrama in court. So it is better to have the bailbond ready, Sir.

Mr. Teng: Alright, I will issue the bailbond, now - You are her guarantor, Atty. Santiago.

Atty. Santiago: Yes Sir.

Ms Luz: What's "probable cause" Atty Santiago, asked Ms. Luz Valdezrama.

Atty Santiago: Ms Luz, "Probable Cause" is such facts and circumstances as would engender a well founded belief that a crime has been committed and that the respondent is probably guilty thereof and should be held for trial -- in our case, the complainant's allegation that Ms Luz executed Deed of Assignment for and in consideration of Php 2,800,000 Pesos, from Mrs Chona Sy, so that Ms Luz will cede, transfer and convey Lot with TCT No. 123456 to Chona Sy and after demand made upon Ms Luz, Ms. Luz failed to cede, transfer and convey to Mrs. Chona Sy, the lot, are facts and circumstances constituting "Probable Cause "and will cause the fiscal to file the case of estafa against Ms. Luz Valdezrama, as probably "guilty" thereof.

Ms Luz: So Atty Santiago what will be our defense?

Atty Santiago: No Defense and I laughed.

Ms Luz: her face sad and apprehensive, said: -- "So we will lose the case. I would rather commit suicide than go to prison, Atty. Santiago. --

Atty Santiago: Don't commit suicide Ms Luz; Just Pray and Pray hard. Don't worry -- Nullum Crimen Nullum Poena / Cine Lege Cine Pena that's our defense --- Nothing is impossible with God.

Ms Luz: So let me have the bailbond today, Mr. Teng, Okay?

Mr. Teng: Don't worry Ms Luz, in any court case, I will trust Atty Santiago with my life..

Atty. Santiago: We will meet here tomorrow at 1 o'clock Ms Luz and go together to the fiscal's office at Kapitolyo, Pasig, Rizal. -- Okay?

Ms Luz: Okay, Atty Santiago

The next day, Luz and I took a ride in my Hillman Hunter car the one paid to me by Col. Magnalonso. II. Ms Luz noticed the car's road worthy performance,

Ms Luz: You have a nice, cute car here –Atty. Santiago.

Atty Santiago: This car was given to me by my client Col. Magnalonso as Attorney's fees, so I use it going to court hearings, have you noticed the air-con, and the radio? New tires, newly painted too.

Ms Luz: Yes, the air-con and the radio were performing well too.

At exactly 2 o'clock in the afternoon we were at the fiscal;s office at Kapitolyo, Pasig, Rizal.

The Fiscal called the case,:

Fiscal: "Complainant Chona Sy versus Respondent, Ms. Luz Valdezrama for Estafa (Swindling), of Php 2,800,000 Pesos ".

Lawyer for Complainant:, We are ready, Mr. Fiscal.

Complainant Mrs. Chona Sy: Here, Sir,.

Atty Santiago: Respectfully appearing as counsel for respondent Ms. Luz Valdezrama, Mr. Fiscal..

Ms. Luz Valdezrama: Respondent, Present, Mr. Fiscal.

Fiscal: Complainant Chona Sy, what's this about Estafa of Php 2,800,000 Pesos you are complaining against respondent Ms. Luz Valdezrama, how did it happen?

Complainant Mrs. Chona Sy: Sir, here is Deed of Assignment, receipt of Ms. Luz Valdezrama. I gave her Php 2,800,000 Pesos for her to give me Lot in a compound along Shaw Boulevard, near Wack-Wack Golf Club, Mandaluyong, Rizal. Ms. Luz gave me no lot -- she must return to me my money, Sir.

Fiscal: What can you say about that Ms. Respondent Luz Valdezrama?

Respondent Ms. Luz Valdezrama: That's not true, Sir.

I whispered to Ms. Luz Valdezrama:

Atty Santiago: Ms. Luz, "You have the right not to testify against yourself".

Ms. Luz Valdezrama: Okay.

Fiscal: Respondent. Ms. Luz Valdezrama, is this your signature?

Fiscal pointing to the signature over the typewritten name Luz Valdezrama - Assignor / Seller Respondent Luz Valdezrama: I have the right not to testify against myself, Sir; --

Fiscal: Respondent, did you give the lot to Complainant?

Respondent: I have the right not to testify against myself, Mr. Fiscal.

Fiscal: The response of respondent show that she had been intelligently counselled, however, the allegation of complainant and her supporting docu- ment, the "Deed of Assignment" are facts and circumstances that make us believe that the crime of estafa has been committed and that the respondent was probably guilty of the same and should be held for trial, but still I will give the respondent ten (10) days within which she may file contro- verting evidence or affidavit, after such period of time I will resolve this complaint with or without such controverting evidence or affidavit.

Respondent Ms. Luz Valdezrama: Thank you Mr. Fiscal.

Fsical: Next Case.

As was stated by the Fiscal, three weeks after, we received the Resolution stating that Estafa case for Php 2,800,000 Pesos was filed against Ms Luz Valdezrama with the Court of First Instance of Pasig, Rizal, bail recommended, Php 40,000 Pesos.

So upon receipt of said Resolution, Ms. Luz Valdezrama and I at once went to the Court of First Instance of Rizal and filed her bailbond for her temporary liberty pending hearing of her case.

I explained to Ms. Luz the ordinary routine and procedure of court hearing --first there will be set a day for arraignment of the accused, wherein, the Clerk of Court will read the charge called the "Information" and will ask the accused to enter her plea -- 'Not Guilty" if the accused will fight the charge -- "Guilty "if the accused has surrendered and will not fight the case anymore. In her case, her answer should be "Not Guilty". I told Ms Luz, 'Not to worry', Just Pray we win the case -- We are fighting for justice, "Nothing is impossible with God".

So I looked in anticipation of the day of the trial as an adventure in exposing an umbilical liar.   .

The Court scheduled at once the Arraignment of the accused with order for continous trial considering the huge amount of Php 2.8 Million Pesos Estafa..

The Court of First Instance of Rizal Branch 234 which will hear the case was housed at Kapitolyo, Pasig, Rizal,

On the day of the hearing, the Court was filled with capacity There were media taking pictures of the courtroom, lawyers waiting for their case to be called and of accused persons.

People were excited to witness a case of estafa with such huge amount involved. Some say the accused was beautiful like movie stars Susan Roces or Amalia Fuentes.

The court proceedings followed, thus:

The Court: Ms Clerk of Court, call the case scheduled for Arraignment and continous trial for today.

The Clerk of Court stood up and announced:

Clerk of Court: "People of the Philippines, plaintiff versus Luz Valdezrama, Accused - Criminal Case No. 234567 For Estafa (Swindling) of Php 2.8 Million Pesos.

I stood up and respectfully bowed a little to the Judge as I said::

Atty. Santiago: Good Morning, Your Honor, I am Atty. Virgilio J. Santiago, respectfully appearing as counsel for the accused, Luz Valdezrama. We are ready for arraignment and continous trial.

The Court: Proceed, Fiscal.

Fiscal: Ms Clerk of Court, kindly read the "Information" (meaning The formal charge) to the accused.

The Clerk of Court,: Reading the "Information" aloud, 'INFORMATION, Criminal Case No. 1234567 For Estafa of Php 2.8 Million Pesos "The Undersigned accuses Luz Valdezrama of the crime of Estafa (Swindling) defined and penalized under Article 315 paragraph _____of the Revised Penal Code of the Philippines. Committed as follows: "That on the 20th day of September 2000 in the Municipality of Mandaluyong, Province of Rizal, and within the jurisdiction of this Honorable Court, you accused Luz Valdezrama received Two Million Eight Hundred Thousand (Ph 2,800,000) Pesos from one Mrs Chona Sy for and in consideration of you ceding, transfering, and conveying unto and in favor of said Chona Sy Lot covered by TCT No. 123456 with area of One Thousand Four Hundred (1.400 Sq.M.) Square Meters, more or less in one compound enclosed by concrete wall situated along Shaw Boulevard, near Wack –Wack Golf Club, in Mandaluyong, Province of Rizal but failed to cede, transfer and convey to said Chona Sy the lot aforementioned and despite demand to return the Two Million Eight Hundred Thousand (Php 2,800,000) Pesos you, accused Luz Valdezrama fail and up to present date continue to fail to cede, transfer and convey the lot to said Chona Sy or to return the money so received to Chona Sy, to the damage and prejudice of Chona Sy.

"CONTRARY TO LAW."

(Sgd) Fiscal _____ Recommended Bail Php 40,000

Clerk of Court: How do you plead, accused Luz Valdezrama?

Accused Luz Valdezrama: NOT GUILTY Madam.

Court: Alright enter a plea of "Not Guity" for the accused. We begin continous trial considering the big amount of estafa involved. I stood up and objected, and said:

Atty Santiago: With due respect to this Honorable Court, we respectfully object to the phrase of this Honorable Court which I quote, "considering the big amount of estafa involved "for the reason your Honor that there was no proof as yet that accused committed "quote Estafa" The amount involved in the case may be big but it has not as yet been proven, your Honor please. --- We request that the phrase "big amount of estafa" be estriken of the record.

Court: Let it stay.

Atty Santiago: Motion for Reconsideration, Your Honor.

Court: Denied. Fiscal proceed with the continous trial.

Ms Luz Valdezrama looked worried.

Fiscal "We call to the witness stand the witness- complainant- Mrs.

Chona Sy as our first witness.

Witness-Complainant Mrs. Chona Sy approached the witnes stand and said:

Mrs. Witness Chona Sy: "Present sir."

Clerk of Court: Please raise your right hand Mrs Witness-"Do you swear to tell the truth, the whole truth, and nothing but the truth, in this case, so help you God?"

Witness Chona Sy: I do Madam.

Fiscal: Madam Witness. Are you the same Complainant, Chona Sy in this case?

Witness Chona Sy: I am, Sir.

Fiscal: Do you know the accused, Ms. Luz Valdezrama in this case?

Witness: Yes Sir, she is Ms Luz Valdezrama, that lady in pink dress, Witness pointing to her.

Clerk of Court: Please stand up Ms. Lady in pink dress. What' s your name, please?

Lady in pink dress: I am Ms Luz Valdezrama, the accused in this case, Madam.

Fiscal: Mrs Witness, why do you know the accused?

Witness: Because I gave her Two Million Eight Hundred Thousand (Php 2,800,000.00) Pesos for her to give me lot in this "Deed of Assignment" -- Witness showing a piece of paper duly notarized with signature at the bottom page over the typewritten name Luz Valdezrama Assignor/Seller, this was notarized, Sir

Fiscal: We request this piece of paper titled "Deed of Assignment "duly notarized on 20th September 2000 be marked as Exhibit "A" and the typewritten name Ms Luz Valdezrama below the page with designation "assignor/Seller" be marked as Exhibit "A-1" and the signature on top of the typewriten name Luz Valdezrama as Exhibit "A-2" and the amount "Two Million Eight Hundred Thousand (Php 2,800,000) Pesos as Exhibit "A-3" and the "Lot TCT No. 123456 as Exhibit A-4" and the name of the Notary Public "illegible" as Exhibit "A-5".

Fiscal continued: and where did you give this amount of Two Million Eight Hundred Thousand (Php 2,800,000.00) Pesos to the accused Luz Valdezrama?

Witness: At the office of the Notary Public, in Mandaluyong, Rizal, on September 20 2000, Sir.

Fiscal: Mrs Witness did the accussed cede, transfer and convey to you the Lot mentioned in the:Deed of Assignment "?

Witness Chona Sy: No Sir.

Fiscal: Did you send any letter of demand for the accused to cede, transfer and convey to you the lot Mrs Witness?

Witness Chona Sy: My lawyer wrote the accused a letter of demand dated September 30 2000 for the accused to return to me the amount of Two Million Eight Hundred Thousand (Php 2,800,000) Pesos I paid her on or before 15th day from receipt of the letter, otherwise, my lawyer will file Estafa case against her. The letter sent by my lawyer was received by her, on the 15th of October but up to now she, the accused, had not return to me the money, Sir. Here is the receipt issued to my lawyer by the post office of Mandaluyong, Rizal, certifying that addressee Ms Luz Valdezrama received the letter on October 15 2000, Sir.

Fiscal: We request the letter of demand dated September 30 2000 be marked as Exhibit "B" and the name of the lawyer who wrote the letter of demand as Exhibit "B-1" and the certification issued by the Mandaluyong Post Office that the addressee received the letter on October 15 2000 be marked as Exhibit "B-2" for the prosecution.

Fiscal: Mrs Witness Did the accused return to you the money demanded by your lawyer?

Witness Chona Sy: No Sir, Up to now she did not return the money.

Fiscal: What did you do next if any?

Witness Chona Sy: I, with my lawyer filed estafa case against accussed Ms. Luz Valdezrama, Sir.

Fiscal: That's all with the witness, Your Honor.

Court: Any Cross Examination, Atty. Santiago?

Atty. Santiago: With the kind permission of the Honorable Court...

Court: Proceed, Atty. Santiago.

Atty. Santiago: Mrs Witness, you did not ask the accused to cede, transfer and convey to you the lot, is that right?

Witness Chona Sy: I did, Sir.

Atty Santiago: Where in the letter of demand did you ask the accused to cede, transfer and convey to you the lot?

Witness: But I did Sir. I telephoned the accused to cede, transfer and convey to me the lot, Sir.

Atty Santiago: There was nothing in black and white you can show that you demanded the accused to cede, transfer and convey to you the lot, right?

Witness: that's right. But I really asked the accused to give me the lot, Sir.

Atty. Santiago: Other than your "say so"you have no paper you can show to us that you did asked the accused to give to you the lot, right?

Witness Chona Sy: That's right, Sir.

Atty Santiago: The truth of the matter was that you did not tell your lawyer to demand that the lot be transferred, ceded and conveyed to you by the accused, correct?

Witness Chona Sy: But I told my lawyer to demand that the accused convey, transfer and cede to me the lot, Sir.

Atty Santiago: Alright Mrs. Sy, will you point to the court where in that letter of demand did your lawyer demand that accused cede, transfer and convey to you the lot.

Witness Chona Sy: There was nothing in that letter Sir. But I told my lawyer to demand that the accused cede, transfer and convey to me the lot, Sir.

Atty Santiago: So why your lawyer did not ask the accused to transfer to you the lot will be your word against the word of the letter of demand of your lawyer, is that not it?

Witness Chona Sy: Cannot answer.

It was noticeable that witness just stuck to her words, although she could not prove it.

Atty, Santiago: Mrs. Sy, did you go to the bank to withdraw money on September 20, 2000?

Witness: No sir;

Atty Santiago: Where were you on September 20 2000?

Witness: At home, sir, afterwards, I went to the office of the Notary Public and paid accused Luz Valdezrama, Php 2,800,000. Pesos, Sir.

Atty Santiago: Where did you get the money to pay the accused Php 2,800,000 Pesos when earlier you told this Honorable Court Mrs Sy you did not withdraw money on September 20 2000?

Witness: I have here the Deed of Assignment, the receipt by the accused it says here "received Php 2,800,000.00 from Mrs Chona Sy to transfer, cede, and convey lot to Mrs Chona Sy Sgd Ms Luz Valdezrama Sir;

Atty Ssantiago: Mrs Witness, my question was "Where did you get the money to pay the accused when earlier you told this Honorable Court Mrs Sy you did not withdraw money on September 20, 2000?

Witness: I did, Sir

Atty Santiago: How could you pay the accused when you did not withdraw money from the bank on september 20 2000 and you did not go out of your house on September 20 2000 Mrs Witness??

Fiscal: Objection your honor, argumentative --

Court: Sustained, Atty Santiago, rephrase your question;

Atty Santiago: Witness Chona Sy will you tell this Honorable Court "how you allegedly paid the accused on September 20 2000 at the office of the Notary Public "?

Witness Chona Sy: While I was at my house on September 20 2000 my debtors came to the house and they paid me their debts. The money they paid me was the money I paid the accused Ms Luz Valdezrama at the office of the Notary Public on September 20 2000, Sir.

Witness Chona Sy then smiled at me like saying "nakalusot"

Atty Santiago: How did you carry the money paid to you by your debtors to the office of the Notary Public, Mrs Sy?

Witness: I put all the money paid to me by my debtors in this bag I am holding now, Sir.

Atty Santiago: That bag you are now holding must be about eighteen inches square, is it not,Mrs Sy?

Witness: I agree. Sir.

Atty Santiago: Did all the money fit in that bag?

Witness: It sure did, Sir

Atty Santiago: Alright, Mrs Witness who were the debtors who paid you at your house on September 20 2000,? what were their names?

Witness: Cannot answer.

Atty. Santiago: "Where do they live,?

Witness: Cannot answer

Atty Santiago: How much did each pay you?

Witness: Cannot answer

Atty. Santiago: What denominations were the money paid to you Mrs Sy, Php 20, 50, 100, 200, 500, 1000 peso bills?

Witness: cannot answer

Atty Santiago: Ms clerk of court please place on record that witness could not tell the Honorable Court the names, the residences, how much money each debtor paid witness-complainant, in what denominations were the money her debtors paid her, whether in Php 20, 50, 100, 500, 1000 peso bills.

Then I continued, --

Atty Santiago: Mrs Witness, what transportation did you take in going to the office of the Notary Public from your house?

Fiscal: Objection, Question is "vague" what transportation did "witness" take in going to the office of the Notary Pubkic "now, yesterday or when"?

Court: Be definite, Atty. Santiago, "When witness go?

Atty. Santiago: Mrs. Witness, what transportation did you take in allegedly going to the office of the Notary Public from your house on September 20 2000?

Witness Chona Sy; I just walked along Shaw Boulevard, about a few blocks, 14 minutes walk from our house.

Atty Santiago: Who were your companion then, Mrs sy?

Witness: No companion, I don't need any companion Sir.

Atty santiago: you mean Mrs, witness you did not have any police escort, or bodyguard or any companion when you walked along shaw boulevard on september 20 2000?

Witness: No need for police escort, or bodyguard or any companion Sir;

Atty Santiago: what time of day was that when allegedly you walked along Shaw Boulevard on September 20 2000?

Witness: I reached the office of the Notary Public about 11 am, so I was walking along Shaw Boulevard about 10:45 in the morning of that day, Sir.

Atty. Santiago: And all the time that allegedly on September 20 2000 you walked along Shaw Boulevard without any police escort, bodyguard, or any companion, you allegedly carried the Two Million Eight Hundred Thousand (Php 2,800,000) Pesos in that bag, is that believable, Madam Wistness?

Witness: Well that was the truth, Sir..

I looked around the court room for reactions. People's faces express various reactions, some faces seem to say ridiculous, the witness' tell incredible story 'imagine carrying Php 2,800,000 Pesos in a bag, without police escort, bodyguard, or any companion, walked along Shaw Boulevard, the scenario of almost daily bag snatching, watch snatching, hold-up and other crimes,';

The faces of other lawyers in court waiting for their turn to be heard of their cases seem to say: the witness was surely telling a big lie. -- that's insanity.

For me, what I wanted to see was the reaction of the judge -- what could the judge be thinking, -- the witness was a liar, no doubt about it, but I must show to the judge that she was lying, by compounding her lies from a "mole hill" to as big as the "Great Wall of China". So I pursued her with my questions:

Atty Santiago: Madam Witness is it not a fact that you did not pay the accused Ms Luz Valdezrama on September 20 2000 at the office of the Notary Public?

Witness Chona Sy: I Did, Sir.

Atty Santiago: Alright, Madam Witness, how did you pay her?

I looked at the Judge, his face expresses disbelief, bordering on annoyance already at the witness who persisted on telling she paid the accussed Two Million Eight Hundred (Php 2,800,000) Pesos money paid to her allegedly by her debtors whose names, residences she could not tell the Court, what denomination, she could not say, and tell incredible story about carrying the huge money in a bag, along Shaw Boulevard, without police escort, bodyguard, or any companion. What other lie could she tell.

Witness: When I reached the office of the notary public it was already 11 in the morning the Deed of Assignment had been duly notarized so I took out from my bag, this bag I am holding now and gave all its money contents to Ms Luz Valdezrama who took the money I paid her then she said she had to go to relieve her of her personal necessity at the coffee shop across the Shaw Boulevard and rushed out of the office of the notary public and she crossed the Shaw Boulevard and went to the coffee shop. She never returned to the office of the Notary Public, Sir. After a long while of waiting for her to return, the Notary Public told me he will go somewhere else so he will have to close his office and he asked me who will pay him the cost of the notarial fee so I asked him how much then he told me Php 200 Pesos only so I paid him and took from him the Deed of Assignment already notarized, Sir.

Atty. Santiago "Mrs Witness, what' was the name of the Notary Public who signed the Deed of Assignment?

Witness: I could not read his signature, Sir.

Atty. Santiago: You did not ask him his name, Mrs. Witness?

Witness: Cannot answer.

Atty Santiago: Where was the office of that Notary Public from whom you took the Deed of Assignment, Mrs Witness?

Witness: Cannot answer

Atty Santiago: How did you know the person from whom you allegedly took the Deed of Assignment was a Notary Public?

Witness: Cannot Answer.

Atty Santiago: You did not see the Notary Public sign that Deed of Assignment as you earlier said when you came to the office of the notary public the Deed of Assignment had been duly notarized already, Correct, Ms Witness?

Witness: That's correct, sir.

Atty Santiago: You also did not see accused Ms. Luz Valdezrama sign that Deed of Assignment, as you earlier testified that when you arrived at the office of the notary public the Deed of Assignment had been notarized already, Correct Mrs Sy?

Witness: Cannot Answer

Atty Santiago: Mrs Witness you do not know who typed this Deed of Assignment, as you testified earlier that when you allegedly came to the office of the notary public, the Deed of Assignment, was already notarized, Correct?

Witness: Cannot answer'

Atty Santiago: Madam Witness, you alleged in your earler testimony that when you came to the office of the Notary Public, the Deed of Assignment was already notarized so you took out all the money contents of your bag and gave it to Ms Luz Valdezrama who took the money and said she had to relieve herself and rushed out of the office, did it not look ridiculous, unimaginable that you will not count the money you allegedly paid to the accused before the alleged notary public -- as in real life transaction, -- so that the Notary Public will witness the payment?

Witness: Cannot Answer.

Atty. Santiago: The fact, Mrs. Witness was there was no transaction - no payment that occurred, Ms Witness, is it not? Please Ms. Witness, may I remind you, deliberate false testimony is punishable by law. Now, What's your answer, Mrs. Witness?

Witness: No Answer.

Atty. Santiago: Ms Clerk of Court, please make it of record, that the witness cannot answer, simple questions asked of her..

Then I continued:

Atty. Santiago: In view of the foregoing facts brought out in the foregoing cross examination, we respectfully move to "Dismiss this Case" on the following legal grounds, Your Honor, please, Number one (1) that there was no payment of Two Million Eight Hundred Thousand (Php 2,800,000) Pesos made by the complainant to the accused, (2) That there was no damage and prejudice suffered by the complainant, having paid nothing; (3) That there was no transaction as alleged "Deed of Assignment" as complainant did not see accused Ms. Luz Valdezrama sign the alleged "Deed of Assignment" and could not prove as to who signed the named Assignor/Seller. (4) That the alleged "Deed of Assignment" had no witnesses to the document, so no witness may be allowed to testify as to who were the parties to it; (5) that the complainant do not know the name of the Notary Public nor the office of the Notary Public; so that no notary public can identify as to the parties to the transaction nor to the transaction itself, so that legally, there was no legal document of Deed of Assignment; (6) That the allegations and testimony of the complainant were incredible, unbelievaable, if not deliberate lies, and product of imagination and (7) That complainant's allegation that the money she paid allegedly Php 2,800,000 Pesos to accused were the very money paid to her by her debtors whose names and residences she could not tell the Court, and how much each debtor paid her, she likewise could not tell this Court, and also she could not tell this Court as to what denominations were the money paid to her by her debtors cast doubt as to its factual veracity and could not be believed (8) That complainant allegedly walked along Shaw Boulevard known to be the usual scenario of bag snatching, hold – up and other crime even during broad daylight, without police escort, or bodyguard, or any companion allegedly carrying Two Million Eight Hundred Thousand (Php 2,800,000) Pesos cash was incredible and insulting to the intelligence of any sane man; (9) That complainant did not count anymore the Php 2,800,000 cash in unknown denomination which allegedly she took out from her bag, which allegedly were payments made to her by the debtors who came to her house on September 20 2000 is unbelievable and cannot be a factual basis of this complaint. That for all these incredible, unimaginable and ridiculous testimony of the complainant, rendered the complaint of the complainant unmeritorious and unworthy of belief hence as per the maxim "Res Ipsa Loquitur - the thing speaks for itself" this case should and must be legally Dismissed being unworthy of credit, unbelievable, untruthful if not utterly a falsehood, unworthy of further consideration, we humbly move once more that the case be dismissed.

Court: What do you say Fiscal.

Fiscal: We object to the motion to dismiss, Your Honor, the Complaint was under oath and so deserves credit --The accused should present her controverting evidence.

Atty Santiago: If your Honor please, where the allegations of the accusation were shown to be incredible to be true, unimaginable and by themselves unmeritorious, and cannot be believed, then it need no proof to controvert it, as the maxim says "Res ipsa loquitur", the thing speaks for itself. And most of all, the accused has in her favor the constitutional right to be presumed innocent, until otherwise proven beyond reasonable doubt.

In our particular case, the complainant failed to prove its accusation even by preponderance of evidence..

As substantially stated by the Honorable Supreme Court, the prosecuting officer is the representative not of an ordinary party to a controversy but of a sovereignty whose obligation to govern impartially is as compelling as its obligation to govern at all and whose interest therefore in a criminal prosecution is not that it shall win a case but that justice shall be done. As such he is in a peculiar and very definite sense the servant of the law, the two fold aim of which is that guilt shall not escape nor innocence suffer. He may prosecute with earnestness and vigor indeed he should do so, but while he may strike hard blows he is not at liberty to strike foul ones.It is as much his duty to refrain from methods calculated to produce a wrongful conviction as to use every legitimate means to bring about a just one. (Suarez vs. Platon).

Wherefore, we once again respectfully move to dismiss the case against accused Ms. Luz Valdezrama, as mandated by the law and the Constitution, and to protect her from unwarranted, untruthful, if not utterly false and unimaginable fantasy of imagination of complainant.

Court: Finding the motion of defense counsel to dismiss the case against accused Luz Valdezrama to be meritorious as the allegations of complainant were in themselves incredible to be true, if not utterly false and bordering on ridiculous imagination and as the accused has in her favor the constitutional right to be presumed innocent until proven guilty beyond reasonable doubt, as prayed for by accused through counsel, the case is hereby ordered "Dismissed". Cancel the bailbond of the accused.

'SO ORDERED. "

Ms. Luz Valdezrama almost jumped with joy.

I looked at the face of the accused Ms Luz Valdezrama, now calm and peaceful. She really looked like movie stars "Susan Roces and Amalia Fuentes" combined, I said to myself.

Ms Luz Valdezrama looked at me and smiled, then she said:

"Thank you Atty Santiago."

Atty Santiago: I told you Luz, "Nothing is impossible with God. "

Then I looked up and uttered, "Thank You Lord God Almighty. Praise be Your Name Forever. "Amen.

Chapter IX
Robbery In Band

(Names* fictional, events true and factual)

I told my mother that I will just hold my "Law Office" at our house so as to accommodate poor people who may need my legal and professional services. I reasoned out to her that if I put up my law office in prestigious location, then I will have to ask for higher fees so as to pay for the rent and the law office staff, such as the room boy, the secretary, the typist, the runner, whereas, in our house I will be a "one man army" lawyer to do everything, A one man lawyer, receptionist, typist, and researcher. I will do everything, I will also be my law office boy, to sweep the floor and clean my office. Then I can afford to ask for lower legal and professional fees as I will not pay rent, pay secretary, receptionist, typist, office boy. My mother laughed at my idea but consented on my plan "for the good of the poor clients, Okay by me", she told me.

So, with the permission of my mother, I re-arranged the furnitures of our living room, put my office table, behind it my swivel chair, two chairs for clients in front of my table, telephone on top of my table, sofa for the 'waiting clients for interview and legal consultation'. That was my "Law Office", which I declared "open" --.

Atty. Santiago: "Open Sesame" let the office 'open' in service for truth and justice, to Honor and Glorify the Lord, God Almighty. Amen."

Then I sat on my swivel chair, took my book on the "Law on Evidence" and re-read it while relaxing.

That was a Sunday morning, I had just been to church. Then, I heard knocks on our door. I peeped out the window and saw many people, some women as old as my mother, some old men as old as my father, and some youngsters, people in their teens, and standing from the crowd was a maiden about 17 years young, beautiful, nice to look at, with innocent looking lovely face, lovely, lovely mestiza with petite and slim body, with fair complexion and with black hair some curling up, bunched up into a "ponytail", "wow how lovely she is" I told myself.

My mother entered the living room from the kitchen and into my "Law Office", open the door, and said to the visitors:

My Mother: Hello, Good Morning:, as she opened the door, Mr. and Mrs. Santos, please come in.

Mr. Santos: We want to consult the legal problem of our son, Junior to Atty. Santiago, Mrs.. Santiago.

My mother: Okay Mr. Santos, come in. My son, Atty. Santiago will attend to you, shortly-

My mother called me to attend to the legal problem of Mr. Santos.

Thus, I said:

Atty. Santiago: Mr. and Mrs. Santos and other nice people, please take your seat.

Everybody took their seat, Mr. and Mrs. Santos took the chairs in front of my office table, some took their seat around the living room, and the lovely mestiza took the sofa directly across my office table. Some just stood by, looking at me..

Mr. Santos opened up the conversation.

Mr. Santos: "Good Morning, I am Mr. Santos, this is my wife, we live down your street, we are neighbors. Our companions are my compadres and their children. My wife and I accompanied your mother to the Insurance company to secure bailbond for you some years ago, you were not yet a lawyer then. just a kid, charged of 'reckless imprudence resulting to frustrated homicide'. And he smiled.

My mother entered the living room of our house, which I made my law office, and joined in the conversion, as she said:

My mother: Yes, we remember your kindness then, Mr. Santos. What can we do for you, Mrs. Santos?

Mrs. Santos: My son, our John Santos, Jr. and his 3 friends, Tom Mallari, son of our compadre Mr. Mallari, here, and Dick and Harry Taruc, sons of our compadre here Mr. Taruc, went to the San Juan Fiesta at San Juan, Rizal last Wednesday, June 24. They did not come back. When we checked the police department of San Juan, we learned they were in the San Juan Municipal jail. My husband will tell you more about it, Atty. Santiago, about what happened, he knew better than I.

Mr. Santos: When our junior and his friends did not come back that night of June 24 I phoned the police department of San Juan about any news on our children. I was told by the police that our sons were in jail for "Robbery in Band" -- imagine -- very embarrassing charge -- is it not Attorney Santiago?

Atty. Santiago: Quite embarrassing, I agree, but what really happened?, Mr. Santos?

Mr. Santos: Our compadres, Mr. Mallari and Mr. Taruc were in our house that time for a visit and were also alarmed when I told them what happened to our sons. So we decided right then and there to go to San Juan Police. At the San Juan Police we were told by our sons that after the fiesta they were planning to go home already so they hailed the taxi "Ben Hur Taxi" and directed the driver to take them to Quirino District Project 2, Quezon City. The usual fare was only Php 12 to 14 pesos, considering that the flag down was only Php 0. 20 and for every 3 electric posts costs 10 centavos only, is that not so, Atty. Santiago?

Atty. Santiago: Well that was the usual cost, considering the distance. What happened next, if any?, I asked.

Mr. Santos: The taxi driver, one Amado Fello told our sons that considering that there were many passengers, he will charge them per contract of Php 50 Pesos from that place N. Domingo Street up to Proect 2, Quirino District, Quezon City, and they will have to pay first as "no flag down". Our sons did not agree and told the taxi driver that they will just get other taxi. But before they could get off the taxi, the driver sped away and unfortunately bumped accidentally or intentionally the police outpost on the N. Domingo Street in front of the Municpal Hall of San Juan and caused it to tumble down. The police manning the outpost came out of the outpost and arrested the driver and our sons, my Junior John, Tom Mallari, son of our compadre Mr. Mallari and Dick and Harry Taruc, sons of our Compadre Taruc for "breach of the peace" for boxing with the taxi driver inside the taxi and were brought to the San Juan Municipal Police Station at Municipal Hall of San Juan.

Mr. Taruc: That Driver was a hustler. When our sons would not want to agree to his "contract" which is illegal as every taxi must use meter to determine the amount a passenger has to pay, this "hustler driver" want to impose his own "contractual way" of taxi fare. He should be reported to the police.

Mr. Mallari: Yes that's correct, the problem is this taxi driver even charged our sons with robbing him of his taxi income. That's really the problem, now the case is in court and it is for us to convince the Judge that our sons did not rob this "hustler" taxi driver.

All the while without my noticing it, I have been looking at the lovely face of that young maiden whom I came to know later to be the youngest daughter of Mr. Mallari, and sister of Tom Mallari, one of the accused.

So much so that when Mr. Mallari suddenly asked me an intriguing question I was almost caught off guard,:

Mr. Mallari: Have you handled a case like robbery before, Atty. Santiago?

I was surprised, and felt slighted momentarily, however, I managed to answer him, as follows:

Atty. Santiago: Actually not yet, Mr. Mallari, however, it is just like a mother giving birth to her first baby -- she does not need to have experience to give birth to her first baby, Is it not?

In the case of a lawyer, all that a lawyer has to do to be successful in handling a case is to have "firm determination to succeed", to focus all effort and devote all his time and energy to study his case and success will come naturally. Of course in my case, I always ask the Great One above for aid and guidance so that I may win the case for truth and justice to prevail, and also, so that I shall not lose the case just because of my "kabobohan" meaning stupidity or lack of knowledge, or lack of skill but because truth and Justice demanded it so, for the greater honor and glory of the Good Lord, God Almighty.

I also ask my clients to pray so that the Judge may not be corrupted by the opposite litigant,. and decide the case according to what is right, and just..

Mr. Taruc: That's nice to hear, Atty. Santiago. You seem more like a pastor than a lawyer.

Atty. Santiago: Well I learned that I am a lawyer not just because I want this job, but more because, I need to pay back other people 's good deeds done to us, I am only a steward to share to others the good graces of the Good Lord God Almighty.

Then I focused my look at Mr. Santos and asked him:

Atty. Santiago: What happened next, Mr. Santos, if any?.

Mr. Santos: I asked the police at San Juan Police Station for copies of the (1) affidavit of arrest of the aresting officers; (2) Affidavit-complaint of the complainant taxi driver; (3) Inventories of items found on the person of the taxi driver and the occupants of the taxi; (4) and affidavits of the occupants, if any -- in our case, our children did not give any statement.

Atty. Santiago: That's good. Were you given the copies of those things you asked for? I asked Mr. Santos.

Mr. Santos: That was last Wednesday evening. I was told the police went to "Kapitolyo" (meaning Capital) of Rizal Province at Pasig, to have the affidavits of the arresting officer and the taxi driver subscribed and sworn to, by the fiscal on duty, and I was told to go the next day to the Court of First Instance of Rizal at "Kapitolyo" at Pasig, Rizal designated to handle the case for hearing and to ask for copies of the court.

So the next day, Thursday, June 25, my compadres Mallari and his youngest daughter, Mercedez, (it was then I learned the name of the lovely maiden who is the personification of all I want in a woman) kid sister of Tom Mallari, and Taruc, the father of Dick and Harry and I, went back to Kapitolyo at Pasig to Branch 234 of the Court of First Instance of Rizal, handling the "Robbery In Band" case against our children and there we asked for copies of the "Information "(meaning, formal charge) and copies of the Joint Affidavit of Arrest of the arresting officers, and the Affidavit-Complaint of the driver, Amado Fello, and the "inventories" of the items found on the person of the driver and the occupants of the taxi, John Santos, my son, Tom Mallari, and Dick and Harry Taruc;

Here are the papers we got from the court, Atty. Santiago. Mr. Santos handed to me the mentioned papers he got from the court.

I took a quick look at the "Information "or formal charge. I noted the bail recommended for each of the accused was Fifteen Thousand (Php 15,000) Pesos for each of the accused, so I commented. –

Atty. Santiago: The bail for each of the accused was set for 15,000 pesos Have you filed bailbond for them, Mr. Santos? I asked.

Mr. Santos: My compadres and I have accumulated Twelve Thousand (Php 12,000) Pesos only which is 20% of Php 60,000 the total amount of bail recommended for the four accused, so I requested the clerk in the court to make a motion for reduction of bail which I signed and she submitted to the court. Last Friday, we went back to the court to find out what happened with our motion for reduction of bail and the clerk sadly showed us our motion for reduction with handwrtten remark from the Judge "Denied" and the amount of P15,000 crossed out and a handwritten amount of P30,000 for each of the accused as bail recommended on top of the "crossed out" amount.

So, filing of bail is already out of our options, sighed Mr. Santos. As he continued:.

"Last Saturday, we, my compadres and I went back to Pampanga province to request our provincemate lawyer to handle the case of our sons, but he asked acceptance fee of Php 20,000 for each of our accused sons, total of Php 80,000, which we cannot afford, so we went back to Manila to seek a Manila lawyer for a lower professional fee, but almost all of the lawyers we have talked to ask acceptance fee of not lower than Php 50,000 for all the accused plus Php 400 appearance fees, postponed or not postponed.

On our way back home, we passed your house and I suddenly remembered some years ago, you were in the same situation we are now in, so I told my compadres, "I think I will ask our neighbor Atty. Santiago to be my lawyer for my son, John" -- then my compadres told me that if I will get my own lawyer then they will just go with me and hire my lawyer as well, so we will have one lawyer only.

Mr. Mallari and Mr. Taruc then joined in the conversation and said:

Mr. Mallari: "We have told you already our predicament, Atty. Santiago, we want to fight our sons' case as we know our sons were innocent of the charge, will you take our sons' case and fight the case for us, Atty. Santiago?"

Mr. Taruc: "We understand you will think that you are being made a "second fiddle" in our selection for a lawyer, but that was not our intention, we are facing a blank wall -- we need a lawyer to fight our case in court, but we do not have the money they charged us, so we cannot pay their fee –"

At this point, my mind was reminded of what my mother had admonished me years ago, "lawyers who charge high profeesional fees, poor clients cannot afford to pay", then I asked myself, "will I be like those lawyers too? "

Then I noticed Mercedez was intently looking at me as if pleading so I thought to myself, with or without "acceptance fees" I will handle the case so as to be near "you" Mercedez.

So, at once I decided, with or without professional fees, I will take their case, but then Mr. Santos, cut my thoughts as he said:

Mr. Santos: "Compadres, here is the envelope containing the Twelve Thousand (Php 12,000) pesos we have accumulated for the bailbond of our sons. We cannot pay bailbond anymore because the bail recommended was increased to Php 30,000 pesos for each accused; We cannot use it to pay for the acceptance fees of lawyers we have talked to because they asked for more than what we have -- I want to give this to Atty. Santiago, for him to use in any way he want just take the case of our sons, do you agree with me?"

Then Mr. Santos faced me and said:

Mr. Santos: "You said in your signbosrd 'Those who have less in life should have more in law, ' Will you accept the defense of our sons please, Atty. Samtiago.?"

Mr. Mallari and Mr. Taruc said: "That's the best we can do to help our sons -- please accept the case of our sons, Atty. Santiago."

I looked around and saw Mrs. Santos, and the elders' faces all apprehensive.. this is their last chance to take a lawyer for their sons and relatives, but my eyes were attracted to lovely "Mercedez".... I saw Mercedez her big round eyes focused on me, as if pleading for me to accept the defense of her older brother -- so beautiful eyes -- ah, Mercedez; "Your wish is my command "

Mr. Santos face turned on me, all eyes focused on me, intently waiting for my response --

Atty. Santiago: "Alright, "Your wish is my Command", I said gazing at Mercedez,"

The faces of Mr. Santos, Mr. Mallari, Mr. Taruc and the elders and Mercedez all brightened up as if saying "Yes, we have Atty. Santiago, we now have a lawyer to fight for us," Then I said, to Mr. Santos, Mr. Mallari and Mr. Taruc,:

Atty. Santiago: "When will be the arraignment of your sons?"

Mr. Santos: "The Judge had scheduled the Arraignment and trial of the case for tomorrow at 8:30 o'clock in the morning session of the court, Atty. Santiago."

Atty. Santiago: "Well then, let us just meet each other in court tomorrow. I will be there at exactly 8:20 in the morning."

Mr. Santos, Mr. Mallari and Mr. Taruc said goodbye and everybody went out. The last one to get out was Mercedez who before she stepped out of the door looked back and saw me still looking at her every move and she smiled at me.

I said to myself, "the personification of all that is beautiful in a woman that I love rolled into one looked back at me and smiled at me – wow., what a wonderful day this is "And I heard wonderful music in the air "ah, when you are in love, "...

After the clients had gone home, I gave to my mother the envelope containing the Twelve Thousand (Php 12,000) Pesos.

My mother was very glad, she tapped me on my shoulder and said:

My Mother: "You see son, you earned this money without much risk, nor effort, in fact it was given to you voluntarily even without your asking for it by Mr. Santos and his group, Mr. Mallari and Mr. Taruc.. Another thing good with this money is that you are given a chance to "make right a wrong". I believe in the innocence of John, Tom, Dick and Harry -- they were framed up by the taxi driver. That you have to prove, for the sake of justice and truth, you have to win this case, as a tribute to the Good Lord for making you a lawyer."

I studied the "Joint Affidavit of Arrest", the "Affidavit-Complaint" of the taxi driver Mr. Amado Fello, and the "Inventory" of things found on the person of the driver, and of each of the occupants of the taxi, Mr. John Santos, Mr. Tom Mallari, and brothers Mr. Dick and Harry Taruc as follows:

"Inventory" of things found on the person of Mr. Amado Fello -- Taxi Drivr "Ben Hur Taxi "

3 pcs 10 peso bills	Php 30.00
5 pcs 5 peso bills;	Php 25.00
5 pcs 1 peso coin	Php 5.00
Total Money peso/coins	Php 60.00
No gun; no knife;	
Nothing follows.	

....

"Inventory" of things found on possession of John Santos

occupant of taxi:

1 pc 10.00 peso bill	Php 10.00
1 pc 5.00 peso bill	Php 5.00
Total money	Php 15.00
No gun; no knife	
Nothing follows.	

....

"Inventory" of things found on possession of Tom Mallari:

Occupant of taxi:
Php 10 pesos 1 ten peso bill;	Php 10.00
Php 5 pesos 1 five peso bill;	Php 5.00
Total Money	Php 15.00
No gun; No knife;	
Nothing follows.	

....

"Inventory" of things found in possession of Dick Taruc,

occupant of taxi:
Php 10 pesos 1 ten peso bill;	Php 10.00
Php 5 pesos 1 five peso bill	Php 5.00
Total Money	Php 15.00
No gun; No knife;	
Nothing follows.	

....

"Inventory" of things found in possession of Harry Taruc,

occupant of taxi::
Php 20 pesos 2 pcs ten peso bill;	Php 20 Pesos
No gun; No knife;	
Nothing follows.	

By Arresting Officers:

PO1 Lauro Gomez	PO2 Frank Ramos
24 June 1971	24 June 1971

End of inventory report

....

The folowing day, very early in the morning, I took my bath and put on my colored dark brown coat and tie and white pants and colored brown shoes.

I bid my mother goodbye and told her:

Atty. Santiago: "Mother I am going to the "Vista "of Robbery In Band at Pasig. I will go now."

And I went out of our house and my Law Office.

I hailed a taxi and directed the driver to bring me to the Kapitolyo, Pasig, Courthouse. It was just about 7:00 o'clock in the morning and we reached Kapiyolyo about 7:30 so I told myself I might as well take breakfast. Fronting the Kapitolyo gate, there was a modest Coffee Shop were lawyers and clients usually sit down for coffee and some talks and greetings and pleasantries.

I took a table where I could have a pleasant view of Kapitolyo so I will always be reminded of my vista. At about 8:00 I have finished my breakfast, so I paid my breakfast and took a liesurely walk towards the courthouse at Kapitolyo.

I was surprised to see many young folks going inside the Kapitolyo so I asked some of them and learned that Miss Universe, in the person of Ms Magie Moran, Philippine Candidate to the Miss Universe pageant who won the "Miss Universe "title will attend the hearing of the "gangrape of a 17 year old folio victim on a "waterbed" scheduled for that morning at the Court of Judge Solidum. So that account for the big crowd going to the courthouse. They want to see Miss Magie Moran, "Miss Universe" in person.

So I walked faster and soon I was at the door of the Courtroom of Judge Solidum.

The door was closed and police were guarding the entrance so that only people who have a "vista "or hearing at that time were allowed inside.

I knocked at the door and told the police who opened the door that I have a vista scheduled for hearing that morning session so I was allowed to come. in. The guard commented:

"You are lucky Sir, many lawyers would like to come in to see Miss Unoiverse but we refused them becuse the room will be overcrowded."

Miss Universe must have heard us talking about her so she looked back at us and smiled at us.

She was really beautiful.

But I told myself, Mercedez to me, is far beautiful than any woman

I have known. All my mind was thinking was her. My eyes searched for Mercedez in the room.

I took my seat in front on the chairs allotted to lawyers who have scheduled hearing of cases for the day.

Soon after I have taken my seat, the Clerk of Court stood in front of the room, addressed the people inside and said:

Clerk of Court: "Complete silence is hereby enjoined.

All cellfon that shall cause unnecessary noise as to disturb the proceedings of the court shall be confiscated and it's holder fined with Five Hundred Pesos (Php 500) and the cellfon shall not be returned until fine has been fully paid; Failure to pay the fine shall be considered in direct contempt and shall be meted one night and one day incarceration in the Municipal Jail of Pasig, Rizal, beginning. from the adjournment of today's hearing."

All were silent.

I looked at Mr. Santos, Mr. Mallari and Mercedez and Mr. Taruc and I saw them muted and their faces expressed fear and respect to the strict rules announced by the Clerk of Court.

Then the Clerk of Court continued:

"Counsels of cases called shall come forward and declare for whom they appear and what case, and whether they are ready or not ready.

All police officers, members of the Armed Forces required to appear in the cases being tried and who shall fail to appear shall be considered in direct contempt for causing unnecessary delay in the dis- pensation of justice prejudicial not only to the prosecution, the defense, the Government, but to the public in general as the usual complaint of people in the hills is the slow grind of justice. "

Then the Clerk of Court announced:

"Now enter the Honorable Judge Arsenio Solidum, Presiding Judge of this court. "(Judge Solidum was later appointed Justice of the Supreme Court).

Judge Solidum entered the court room with solemn face, then ordered the Clerk of Court to call the No, l in the cases scheduled for hearing.

Clerk of Court: People of the Philippines, plaintiff, CriminalCase No. 3456789 For: "Gangrape of 17 year old folio victim on waterbed, versus George Andal*, Dieatri Mafian *, Tano Ching,*, Rex Curtis* and Felis Sano * (name *fictitious, but incidents factual), Accused.

All accused stood up.

Judge Solidumm: Where are your Counsels?

Accused,: We were told our lawyers will be coming to the Court', Sir.

Judge Solidum: Where are the counsels for the accused?

Lawyers for the accused: We are ready your honor.

Judge Solidum: No, that was not my question. I asked "where are the counsels for the accused."?,

All was quiet. There was a confrontation coming up.

Judge Solidum continued,: Were you not here when the Clerk of Court announced the rule of this court on the matter of appearing counsel to come to the front and state for whom he or she is appearing, for and what case and whether he or she is ready or not ready?

Lawyers for the accused: We are sorry Your Honor, that was not the way in the other courts we have appeared.

Judge Solidum: Precisely that rule was announced by the Clerk of Court so that we can speed up the proceedings in this court so as to have no back-logs.

Lawyers for the accused: We are sorry, Your Hnor, there will be no repetition of our mistake, po. I looked back to my clients, especially at Mercedez and noted they were all stiff -like statues in awful fear.

Judge Solidum: Alright, Fiscal proceed to trial. Call your witnesses.

Fiscal: We are presenting the Police who arrested the accused in this case -- PO2 Bien Tanio, for our first witness.

After a long while of waiting, the Fiscal said:

Fiscal: Our witness PO2 Bien Tanio was not in court, Your Honor. We will have to request for a resetting of the case.

Judge Solidum: Fiscal, remember this case "Gangrape of 17 year old maiden on a waterbed" is a heinous crime, and if proven by evidence required by the law, the accused may be meted with the highest possible penalty, yet the accused has also the right to speedy trial which must be respected, so, we will wait for your witness PO2 Tanio to arrive in court, then we will continue with the hearing of the case, meanwhile Ms. Clerk of Court, call the No. 2 case scheduled for arraignment and hearing for today.

Clerk of Court: People of the Philippines, plaintiff, for Robbery In Band, (In America this is similar to Highway Robbery), Criminal Case No. 432189 - versus -- John Santos,*, Tom Mallari*, and brothers Dick* and Harry* both surnamed Taruc*, Accused, for Arraignment and trial.

I immediately stood up and approached the front, while saying:

Atty. Santiago: Good Afternoon, I am Atty. Virgilio Santiago, respectfully appearing as counsel de parte for all the accused in this case. All the accused are detention prisoners for failure to file bail due to financial restraints. We are ready. Your Honor.

Court: Alright, Clerk Of Court, read the "Information to the accused."

Clerk of Court: Accused John Santos, Tom Mallari, brothers Dick and Harry Taruc, do you understand English? The "Information" is written in English, If you do not understand English, we will call an interpreter.

Accused, John Santos, Tom Mallari, Dick Taruc and Harry Taruc, all said: We are all graduates of business administration, we understand English, Madam.

Clerk of Court: Okay then, "Accused John Santos, Tom Mallari. Dick Taruc and Harry Taruc, I will now read the "Information" as follows:

"The undersigned accuses John Santos, Tom Mallari, Dick and Harry Taruc., of committing unlawfully, feloniously, and illegally, the crime of robbery in band in that on the '24ᵗʰ day of June 1971 in the evening thereof, the said accused acting together, with one common design, with the aid of a knife 7 inches long, did then and there in the Municipality of San Juan, within the jurisdiction of this Honorable Court, the said accused threatened and pointed the said knife to the neck of the taxi driver Amado Fello with Professional driver's license No. 78654 issued by the Land Transportation Office, Apalit, Pampanga valid until December 31, 1971, driver of Ben Hur Taxi with Plate No. 5678 series 1971 and did then and there took away and robbed the said driver Amado Fello the sum of Six Hundred (Php 600) Pesos all earnings of the taxi and the taxi company to which it is registered."

"Contrary to Law".

Clerk Of Court: How do you plead? Question to the accused.

Accused John Santos, Tom Mallari, Dick Taruc and Harry Taruc, declared: "NOT GUILTY, Madam."

Court: "Alright, Enter "Not Guilty" for all the accused. Fiscal, proceed with the hearing ", --

Fiscal: "We call the arresting officer PO1 Lauro Gomez of San Juan Outpost at N. Domingo Street, San Juan, Rizal. as our first witness."

Clerk of Court: "PO1 Lauro Gomez, not in court, Your Honor."

Judge Solidum presiding judge of the Court declared: "For failure of PO1 Lauro Gomez to appear in court for todays hearing of which hearing he was duly notified "Order" is hereby given in open court for the Bailiff to arrest for "direct contempt of court" the said police officer PO1 Lauro Gomez and bring said person to court and place him under legal custody of the court until his testimony has been terminated in accordance with law. So Ordered.";

Judge Solidum, then continued:

"Ms. Clerk of Court, make direct communication to the San Juan Police Department to render whatever assistance necessary to aid Bailiff to effect the arrest of PO1 Lauro Gomez and carry out this Order. No allowance, salary and/or other emoluments of the office shall be given said PO1 Lauro Gomez until this Order shall have been cancelled in accordance with law. Make the communication in writing I will sign it after adjournment of this hearing. Remember: ' No One is above the law'.

I said to myself, this Judge Solidum is really brave and strict - but fair.

Bailiff: Yes, Your Honor.

And he immediately went out to carry the 'order' of the Court.

Fiscal: In view of the absence of the witness for the prosecution, we will be constrained to ask for a postponement of this case, Your Honor.

I immediately stood up and interposed my objection:

Atty. Santiago: Objection Your Honor, my clients are detention prisoners and are entitled to speedy trial -- The prosecution can present other witnesses if they have other witnesses but they have no right to violate the constitutional right of the accused to speedy trial just because of the absence of their witnesses—We demand for the Dismissal of the case for "Non Prosequi" or failure to prosecute, Your Honor.

Court: That's right; The accused are entitled to speedy trial. Considering that the accused are detention prisoner, the more right they have to swift justice. Fiscal, present other witness for the prosecution.

Mercedez looked at me with her round black eyes and smiled at me which Inspired me to be my best.

Mr Santos and Mr. Mallari and Mr. Taruc' s face beam up with my alertness and fighting mood.

At that point in time, the Bailiff entered the courtroom with PO1 Lauro Gomez, and announced:

Bailiff,: As per Order of the Honorable Court, this representation has brought the person of PO1 Lauro Gomez and he is ready to be dealt with under the law.

Fiscal: In that case Your Honor, we will present PO1 Lauro Gomez as our first witness for the prosecution.

Judge Solidum: Alright Mr. PO1 Lauro Gomez, what can you say for yourself? Explain yourself.

PO1 Lauro Gomez: Your Honor, I and PO2 Frank Ramos, were already inside the Kapitolyo walking towards the court, when a man snatched the bag of an old woman ahead of us. We gave chase and apprehended the snatcher and brought him to the Kapitolyo Police Station for proper investigation by the Station. As we have to leave the station for court duty,. the police station told us to come back after lunch and copy of the police report will be issued to us for presentation to this Court.

Judge Solidum: So in that case, I commend you PO1 Lauro Gomez and PO2 Frank Ramos for your good performance of duty in catching the snatcher - Ms. Clerk of Court, Cancel my Order about the arresat of PO1 Lauro Gomez, when he submit the police report about the snatcher. Are you ready to testify now, PO1 Gomez?

PO1 Lauro Gomez: Ready, Your Honor, Sir.

Fiscal: Take the witness stand, please.

Ms Clerk of Court: PO1 Lauro Gomez, please raise your right hand and swear: "Do you swear to tell the truth, the whole truth and nothing but the truth, in this case, so help you God?:

PO1 Lauro Gomez,: I do, Madam.

I looked at Miss Universe, still waiting for the hearing of the "Gangrape of the 17 year old maiden on the waterbed". She was really beautiful.

Then I looked at Mercedez, the youngest child of Mr. Mallari and the kid sister of Tom Mallari, my heart jumped and danced, with blissful joy. For me she looked far more beautiful than any other woman in the courtroom.

Mercedez noticed I was looking at her, she smiled at me -- ahh that innocent smile, I said to myself..

Clerk of Court: Your witness, Mr. Fiscal.

Fiscal: Mr. Witness, where were you between the hour of 6 and 10 in the evening of June 24 1971?

Witness: I was with PO2 Frank Ramos, performing my duty as police officer, we were both manning the police outpost at N. Domingo street, in front of the Municipal Hall of San Juan, Rizal, Sir.

Fiscal: Was there any unusual incident that happened that night, Mr. Witness?

Witness: At about 9 in the evening a taxi bumped our police outpost that caused us to tumble so we, PO2 Frank Ramos and I got up and arrested the driver of the taxi named "Ben Hur" taxi, for bumping our police outpost and the occupants of the taxi and the taxi driver for breach of the peace for quarelling against each other and brought them to the Police Station at the Municipal Hall of San Juan. Sir.

Fiscal: Do you remember having executed an affidavit of arrest regarding that incident?;

Witness: PO2 Frank Ramos and I, PO1 Lauro Gomez executed Joint Affidavit of Arrest of the driver of the "Ben Hur Taxi" for reckless driving resulting to bumping the Police Outpost of San Juan at N. Domingo street, and of breach of the peach against the driver of the taxi and the occupants of the taxi, John Santos, Tom Mallari, Dick Taruc and his brother Harry Taruc, for breach of the peace, for fighting against each other inside the taxi. Sir. We also attached to our joint affidavit the "Inventory "of the things we found in the persons we arrested as annex of our Joint Affidavit of Arresat, Sir.

Fiscal: Showing you Mr. Witness original of the joint affidavit with attached "Inventory" executed by PO2 Frank Ramos and PO1 Lauro Gomez, what relation has this with the joint affidavit and "Inventory" you earlier mentioned relative to this case?

Witness: This was the original of our Joint Affidavit of Arrest and with attached "Inventory", Sir, there below the page was my signature and the signature of PO2 Frank Ramos, we both signed in the presence of each other. Sir.

Fiscal: Mr. Witness, do you affirm and confirm the truth of all the things and matters stated in your Joint Affidavit and its attached "Inventory"?

Witness: Yes Sir., I do.

Fiscal: We request the Joint Affidavit of Arrest identified by the witness as their Joint affidavit, be marked as Exhibit "A" and the attached "Inventory" as Exhibit "B"; the signature of PO1 Lauro Gomes as Exhibit "A-1"; the Signature of PO2 Frank Ramos as Exhibit "A-2"; and the Signature of PO1 Lauro Gomez in the attached "Inventory" as

Exhibit "B-1" and the Signature of PO2 Frank Ramos as Exhibit "B-2"; All for the Prosecution.

Fiscal: Mr. Witness please look around the courtroom and point to the persons you arrested, if they are in court?

Witness: There they are, Sir. Witness pointing to the driver Amado Fello and to the accused, John Santos, Tom Mallari, Dick and Harry Taruc..

Ms. Clerk of Court: The persons pointed to by the witness gave their names as, Amado Fello, the driver of the "Ben Hur" taxi; John Santos, Tom Mallari, Dick and Harry Taruc, passengers of the "Ben Hur "taxi, Your Honor;

Fiscal: That's all with the witness. Your Honor.

Court: Atty. Santiago, any cross examination?

I stood up and bowed a little to the Honorable Judge, and I said:

Atty. Santiago: With the kind indulgence of the Honorable Court, Mr. Witness, I am showing to you duplicate original of your Joint

Affidavit of arrest with attached "Inventory" marked Exhibits "A"; A-1" and "A-2" and "B" and "B-1" and "B-2" issued to us by the Clerk of Court, please examine them thoroughly, and tell us, is there anything you would want to change, delete or alter in it after you have sworn on it?

Witness: None Sir.

Atty. Santiago: We request that the Joint Affidavit of Arrest with it''s markings be marked for the defense as Exhibit 1 and the signature of PO1 Lauro Gomez be marked as Exhibit 1-1 and its attached "Inventory" with its markings be marked as Exhibit 2 and the signatures of PO1 Lauro Gomez as Exhibit 2-1 and the signature of PO2 Frank Ramos on the Joint Affidavit of Arrest be marked for the defense as Exhibit 1-2 and the signature of PO2 Frank Ramos on the attached:"Inventory" be marked as Exhibit 2-2. That's all with the witness, thank you,, Your Honor.

Court: That's all, Atty. Santiago?

The Judge shook his head, and turned his head left to right, right to left, in disbelief.

Fiscal: We are presenting our second witness, PO2 Frank Ramos, Your Honor, please--.

Frank Ramos: Here sir, as he approached the witness stand.

Clerk of Court: Please raise your right hand and answer-- PO2 Frank Ramos, do you swear to tell the truth, the whole truth and nothing but the truth in this case, So help you God?

PO2 Frank Ramos: "I do, Madam".

Ms Clerk of Court: Your Witness, Mr. Fiscal.

Fiscal: "Mr. Witness, where were you between 6 and 10 in the evening of June 24, 1971"?

Witness Frank Ramos: PO1 Lauro Gomez and I, PO2 Frank Ramos were performing our duty as police officers manning the police outpost at N. Domingo Street, San Juan, Rizal, fronting the Municipal Hall of San Juan, Rizal between the hour of 6 and 10 when our outpost was bumped by a taxi named "Ben Hur" Taxi, that caused us to tumble down. We got up and arrested the driver of the taxi for "Reckless Imprudence resulting to bumping the Police Outpost of San Juan Police at N. Domingo Street, San Juan, Rizal ", and the passengers of the taxi for fighting with the driver of the taxi for "Breach of the Peace", Sir.

Fiscal: Mr. Witness what else did you do if any?

Witness: We "frisked the driver and the other arrested persons for 'deadly weapon and or illegal items in their possession" and made an inventory of the things found in their possession. Then we brought them all to the Municipal Hall of San Juan for further investigation, Sir.

Fiscal: "Mr. Witness, do you remember having executed any affidavit in connection with this incident "?

Witness: PO1 Lauro Gomez and I, PO2 Frank Ramos executed a Joint Affidavit of Arrest and its attached "Inventory" of things found in possession of the persons arrested, regarding the arrest of Amado Fello, the taxi driver, and the occupants of the taxi, John Santos, Tom Mallari, Dick Taruc and his brother Harry Taruc who were fighting with the driver of the taxi Amado Fello, and charged them with breach of the peace.

Fiscal: Mr. Witness., showing you this one page Joint Affidavit of Arrest with signatures at the bottom page over the typewritten name PO2 Frank Ramos, what relation has this with the Joint Affidavit of Arrest and attached "Inventory" of things found in possession of the persons you mentioned you arrested?

Witness: This was the duplicate original copy of the Joint Affidavit of Arrest and its attached "Inventory" we, PO1 Lauro Gomez and I, PO2 Frank Ramos executed. There was my signature at the bottom of the page on top of the typewritten name PO2 Frank Ramos, there was also the signature of PO1 Lauro Gomez on top of the typewritten name PO1 Lauro Gomez, Sir. We signed together.

Fiscal: Mr. Witness, do you affirm and confirm the truth of all the contents of this Joint Affidavit and its attached "Inventory" of things found in possession of the persons arrested?

Witness: Yes Sir, I do.

Fiscal: Mr. Witness, please look around the courtroom and point to the persons you mentioned in your Affidavit of Arrest you arrested, if they are here?

Witness: There they are, the driver of the "Ben Hur" taxi, Amado Fello, and the passengers of the taxi, John Santos, Tom Mallari, Dick and Harry Taruc, Sir.

Clerk of Court: Your Honor, the persons pointed to by the witness when asked of their names, answered: Amado Fello, driver of "Ben Hur "taxi, John Santos, Tom Mallari, Dick Taruc and Harry Taruc, passengers of the taxi, Sir;

Fiscal: We request that the Joint Affidavit of Arrest

Identified by the witness as his Joint Affidavit of Arrest as well as the signature at the bottom of the page as his, be marked as Exhibit "double "AA"; "AA-1" for his signature and the "Inventory" likewise identified by the witness be marked as Exhibit double "BB" and the signature of PO2 Frank Ramos as "BB-1"; All for the Prosecution.

Fiscal: That's all with the witness, Your Honor.

Court: Any Cross. Atty. Santiago?

I immediately stood up and bowed to the Judge, as I said:

Atty. Santiago: Thank you Your Honor, Mr. Witness, showing you defense duplicate original of the Joint Affidavit of Arrest and its attached "Inventory" with its markings, will you please go over it and tell us if you have anything you want to change in it, or add anything on it, or delete anything from it after you have sworn on it?

Witness: There's nothing I want to add in it, nor delete from it, nor change in it, Sir.

Atty. Santiago: We request that the Joint Affidavit of Arrest and its attached "Inventory" with its markings be marked also for the defense as Exhibit 2 for the Joint Affidavit, Exhibit 2-2 for the signature of PO2 Frank Ramos, Exhibit 2-1 for the signature of PO1 Lauro Gomez for the defense. That's all with the witness. Thank You, Your Honor.

Court: "What happened, Atty. Santiago, you have adopted the Joint Affidavit of Arrest as well as the Inventory of the police. What more do you expect?".

There was a hush-hush whispers of comment, pros and con in low tone heard in the court. The accused' fathers Santos, Mallari, and Taruc, were all alarmed at the adverse remark of the Judge.

Mercedez looked worried.. What happened with our lawyer, it seems he was not fighting for our case anymore.

Fiscal: We call to the witness stand the complainant taxi driver to identify the accused, robbers.

I stood at once and cried out "Objection" loud and clear.

Atty. Santiago: Objection Your Honor, the statement of the Hon. Fiscal as quote "we call the complainant taxi driver to 'identify' the accused – "robbers" ' was improper, ' and should be removed from the records as the "accused "your Honor are under "trial" as yet, and to call them as 'robbers' is a mere conclusion of law without legal basis as yet in fact and in law, therefore we move that the improper phrase be striken off the records lest "it poison and mislead" the pure mind of the court.

Court: Alright, strike out the phrase objected to by Atty. Santiago.

I caught Mercedez looking at me and as I looked at her she caught me looking at her too. She smiled at me as if saying "me tama ka sa akin, ano?"

Taxi Driver Complainant: Here, present, Sir.

Clerk of Court: Complainant taxi driver please raise your right hand, and swear-- "Do you swear to tell the truth, the whole truth, and nothing but the truth in this case, So help you God"?

Witness-: I do. Madam.

Clerk of Court: "Please state your name, age, sex, residence, civil status and other personal circumstances".

Witness: "I am Amado Fello, 45 years old, driver by occupation, male, married, residing at 1234 Blumentritt street, San Juan, Rizal, Sir. "

Fiscal: "Your Honor, we are presenting the witness to prove that he was the complainant-witness against the accused, John Santos, Tom Mallari, Dick Taruc and Harry Taruc; that the crime of robbery in band was committed on June 24 1971 at San Juan Rizal, within the jurisdiction of this Hnorable Court; That the accused robbed complainant of P600 pesos; that the complainant can identify the robbers as the accused.

May we proceed, Your Honor?"

Court: What do you say Atty. Santiago?

Atty. Santiago: We will object in the course of the examination to improper questions, misleading and leading questions, as well as immaterial and irrelevant questions and other objectionable questions "unfair" to a just and fair hearing, Your Honor, Thank you.

Court: Alright, proceed Mr. Fiscal.

Fiscal: Mr. Witness, are you the same complainant, taxi driver, Amado Fello*, in this case of Robbery In Band against the accused John Santos*, Tom Mallari*, Dick Taruc * and his brother Harry Taruc*?

Witness: I am, Sir.

Fiscal: Mr. Witness, where were you on June 24 1971?

Witness: I was driving a "Ben Hur" taxi for hire in San Juan Municipality.on June 24 1971, Sir

Fiscal: Will you tell this Honorable Court, what unusual incident happened to you on that day, if any.

Witness: At about 9 in the evening, of June 24 1971 I was driving the taxi "Ben Hur" with plate no. 34567 along N. Domingo Street when 4 persons hailed my taxi. I stopped my taxi and as they boarded the taxi they told me to bring them to Project 2, Quirino District, Quezon City. As soon as they have boarded the taxi they brought out a kitchen knife and held me up saying "Hold-Up "ito, we want your money" - then they pointed the knife at my neck and took all my money, Php 600 in all. I felt so afraid that I sped my taxi and bumped the outpost of the San Juan Police at N. Domingo Street, - then we fought each other and the police caught us all and brought us inside the Municipal Hall where the police frisked us all and the police executed their Joint Affidavit of Arrest and I executed my Affidavit-Complaint. At the Municipal Hall police department I came to know the names of the persons who 'hold-up ' me and robbed me as John Santos, Tom Mallari, Dick Taruc and his brother Harry Taruc, Sir.

Fiscal: Mr. Witness, please look around the courtroom and tell the court if the persons whom you told us quote "hold-up me' are in court?

Witness: They are in court, Sir

Fiscal: Point them to the court, Mr. Witness.

Witness: "There they are, Sir, pointing to the accused, John Santos, Tom Mallari, Dick Taruc and Harry Taruc.

Clerk of Court: "Your Honor, the persons pointed to by the witness, when asked of their names, answered: John Santos, Tom Mallari, Dick Taruc and Harry Taruc.

Fiscal: Showing you this Affidavit-Complaint of one Amado Fello with signature on top of the typewritten name Amado Fello, what can you say about it?

Witness: That was my Affidavit-Complaint, and the signature there was my signature, Sir.

Fiscal: Showing you this Affidavit of Arrest by the police, what can you say about this?

Witness: That was the affidavit of arrest of the police manning the police outpost who arrested us. There was my signature, Sir.

Fiscal: We request the Affidavit of Arrest of the police identified by the witness to be marked as Exhibit "B" and the signature pointed to by the witness as his signature be marked as Exhibit "B-1" and the Affidavit - Complaint of Amado Fello be marked as Exhibit "A" and the signature on top of the typewritten name Amado Fello on it be marked as Exhibit "A-1" and the amount Six Hundred ((Php 600) Pesos be encircled and marked as Exhibit "A-2". And the names John Santos, Tom Mallari, Dick Taruc and Harry Taruc named in the affidavit - complaint as the persons who robbed the witness be encircled and marked as Exhibit "A-3, A-4, A-5, A-6";

Fiscal: "That's all with the witness. "

Court: Any Cross-examination, Atty. Santiago?

Atty. Santiago: With the kind indulgence of the Honorable Court.

Court: Proceed, Atty. Santiago.

Atty. Santiago: Mr. Witness, how long have you been a taxi driver for "Ben Hur Taxi "?

Witness: Almost a year, Sir.

Atty. Santiago: On June 24 1971 what hour in the morning did you start driving that "Ben Hur Taxi"?

Witness: I started at about 5 in the early morning, Sir.

Atty. Santiago: And you stopped at what hour of that day?

Witness: I stopped at 12 PM to eat lunch, Sir.

Atty. Santiago: And when did you start driving again the "Ben Hur Taxi: Mr. Witness?

Witness: I started driving the taxi again at 1 PM. It was "Fiesta" many passengers, Sir.

Atty. Santiago: You testified earlier that the money taken from you was Php 600 pesos, all this was money of the taxi, was that correct?

Witness? Yes sir.

Atty. Santiago: You mean from 5 in the early morning to the time you were allegedly held-up your taxi already earned php 600?

Witness: That's true, about ll in the monring of that day I had already earned Php 200 pesos, I gave my wife php l00 pesos for lunch and dinner as it was "Fiesta" then I ate lunch at 12 PM, then by l PM I am again on the street to earn more money l PM to 9 PM is 8 hours, Php 500 to 600 pesos is easy to earn if you know how, Sir.

Atty. Santiago: Alright, so you have earned Php 200 as early as 11 am and you gave your wife l00 pesos -- that was money of the taxi you gave her, was it not?

Witness: Yes Sir. But I am entitled to commission on that money, Sir.

Atty. Santiago: Still that was money of the taxi, until you have remitted it to the Taxi Company and your commission paid to you, is it not, Mr. Witness?

Witness: Correct Sir.

Atty. Santiago: Is it possible Mr. Witness that you gave more than One Hundred (Php 100) Pesos to your wife considering that it was "fiesta time"?

Witness: Possible.

Witness smiled--

Atty. Santiago: Is it also possible that you gave all money earned by the taxi to your wife, and charged it to the alleged "robbers", Mr. Witness?

Witness: That"s not true.

Atty. Santiago: According to you, you gave one hundred Pesos to your wife considering it was "fiesta time", Is it possible that later in the afernoon, say 3:00 o'clock you returned to your house and gave another bunch of earnings of the taxi, say 200 Pesos more to your wife consider- ing that many passengers were riding taxi during that time Mr. Witness,?

Then I look at the Judge the "possibility "was on the face of the judge.

Atty. Santiago: How many passengers have hired your taxi from 5 in the morning up to the time you bumped the police outpost Mr. Witness, ten passengers, twenty?

Witness: Maybe about 30 passengers. Sir.

Atty. Santiago: So you have flag down your taxi meter at least 30 times, correct,?

Witness: Correct Sir.

Atty. Santiago: And all those flag downs reflected on the meter, Mr. Witness?

Witness: Must be, Sir

Atty. Santiago: Did you flag down all those 30 passengers, Mr. Witness? Of Course we can open your taxi meter for verification.

Witness: Did not answer

Atty. Santiago: Why don't you answer, Mr. Witness?

Witness: Cannot answer.

Atty. Santiago: Where did you sign this Affiavit-Complaint Exhibit "A"? Mr. Witness?

Witness: I signed my affidavit-Complaint at San Juan Municipal Police Station at San Juan Municipal Hall. Sir.

Atty. Santiago: Mr. Witness when did you sign it?

Witness: June 24 1971 about 10 PM, Sir.

Atty. Santiago: When did you swear on your affidavit before the fiscal?, the administering Officer?

Witness: What fiscal?, I have not seen any Fiscal at anytime, at the Municipal Hall, Sir..

Atty. Santiago: The whole day or night of June 24 1971 you have not seen any fiscal, Mr. Witness, is that what you mean?

Witness: The whole day and night of June 24 1971 I have not seen any Fiscal, Sir.

Atty. Santiago: So, where did you swear on your Affidavit-Complaint? Who administered your oath?

Witness: I did not swear on that Affidavit-Complaint, Sir..

Atty. Santiago: Mr. Witness When you and the other occupants of the taxi were arrested by the San Juan Police manning the police outpost at N. Domingo street, San Juan., Rizal, were you frisked for whatever you have on your person then?

Witness: That's correct Sir.

Atty. Santiago: What about the other occupants arrested were they also frisked?

Witness: The passengers were also frisked, Sir.

Atty. Santiago: How far away were you from the police and the persons they were frisking or searching?

Witness: About 3 meters Sir'

Atty. Santiago: What did you do while the police were searching the passengers?

Witness: Nothing Sir.

Atty.Santiago: Did you say, anything?

Witness: Nothing, Sir.

Atty. Santiago: Did you not tell the police "watch out they have a knife" or "they were armed "?

Witness: No answer.

Atty. Santiago: Did you not tell the police "they have my money Php 600."

Witness; No answer.

Atty. Santiago: At this point Your Honor please, we respectfully move to dismiss the case against the accused John Santos, Tom Mallari, Dick Taruc and Harry Taruc on the following legal grounds: (1) The law requires that the accused shall be convicted beyond reasonable doubt nothing less than "beyond reasonable doubt" however when the Complainant so clearly declared during the Cross-examination that he gave one hundred pesos income of the taxi to his wife as it was fiesta time, and the complainant declared "possible" as an answer to a follow-up question as to whether it is possible that "he" gave more than one hundred pesos to his wife a "doubt", a definite doubt that complainant may have given more monsey of the taxi to his wife existed; add to this the follow-up question "is it possible that you returned to your house and gave your wife another bunch of money say P300" to which the complainant cannot answer anymrore; (2) That the complainant admitted there was no Affidavit-Complaint when he definitely declared that "he did not swear" on the Affidavit-Complaint. Then there was no basis for the resolution giving rise to an Information which caused the prosecution of the accused. The prosecution of the accused without any Affidavit-Complaint duly executed is a fatal violation of the constitutional right of the accused to procedural due process, violation of which cannot be cured because it rsulted to the death of a right which cannot be revived. (3) that the complainant did not say anything to "warn" the police frisking the passengers of the taxi "that the passengers were holduppers and have a kitchen knife 7 inches long, if truly they have a kitchen knife which will endanger the lives of the police "gives doubt as to the truth of complainant's allegation that the passengers indeed have a kitchen knife, and shows that complainant made an unrelieable story of "hold-up me" story or a "Frame up story" just to charge the accused with the money complainant gave to his wife. (4) Even the Affidavit of Arrest of the police evidence that the charge they leveled to the occupants of the taxi was "mere" "Breach of the

Peace" as the inventory of the things police found on the person of the occupants of the taxi merely show some money very small in amount from what was being claimed by the complainant; Also the inventory as annexed "A" of the Affidavit-of Arrest by the police show "No Gun: No knife". Thus as a whole, the complainant 's allegation suffer from an anemic of evidence which could not even prove a preponderance of evidence.

Whereas the accused have in themselves the constitutional guarantee of presumption of innocence.

Wherefore there is no sense in further proceeding in futility wasting the "time, money and effort "of the government which could be better put to otherwise beneficial and concrete project.

Court: What do you say Fiscal?

Fiscal: Objection, Your Honor. The accused should present "controverting evidence".

Court: No more. The accused are presumed to be "innocent" under the fundamental law of the land and the charge was not proven even by an iota of evidence.

Wherefore, Finding merit to the motion to dismiss filed by accused through counsel, the Case is hereby ordered "Dismissed".

Release the accused from further confinement, unless held on some other legal ground.

"So Ordered."

The accused embraced each other with joy

Mr. Santos, Mr. Mallari and Mr. Taruc embraced their sons.

Mercedez embraced me and whispered, "Thank you. I know you will look for me, I will wait for you".

I looked up and uttered my fervent prayer "Thank you Lord God Almighty. Praise be Your Name Forver." Amen.

Chapter X

The Wedding

(Names*fictional/events true)

Early in the morning of the Sunday after the successful dismissal of the Robbery in Band Case Mr. Santos, Mr. Mallari and his youngest daughter Mercedez, the kid sister of Tom Mallari, and Mr. Taruc, came to our house the living room of which I made my "Law Office". My mother ushered them in.

My mother opened up the conversation saying:

My mother: Good Morning to you all, Please come in.

Mr. Santos: We came early to invite you Mrs. Santiago and your son, Atty. Santiago to have lunch with us and our families and elders,. to celebrate our sons' release and "winning "their embarrssing case leveled against them by that "hustler" taxi driver. Our elders from the province came to our house to celebrate with us. "Pwede po ba? Mercedez will fetch you "po" as soon as the table is ready.

My Mother: We will be glad to celebrate with your families the early release of your sons., Mr. Santos, Mr. Mallari, and Mr. Taruc. And whose daughter is this beautiful young lady, what"s your name?

Mercedez: I am Mercedez Mallari "po", youngest daughter of Mr. Mallari and youngest sister of Tom Mallari. I am already 17 po.

Then my mother added,:

My Mother: Mercedez, a beautiful name for a beautiful young lady; Then my mother turned to Mr. Santos and said --

My Mother: Mr. Santos. We will not cook lunch, anymore, we will just wait for Mercedez, is that it?

Mr. Santos and the others replied: That's right, po. Mrs. Santiago.

My mother looked at me. Her face shone with joy and happiness, her eyes seemed to tell me, "see my son, how respectable you are now. Thanks God He made you a lawyer. "

Then the group went home. But before Mercedez could step out of our door, she looked back and caught me still looking at her. She gigled and her face blushed as she smiled at me, as if saying "me gusto ka sa akin ano?, meaning, you like me, yes?".

I looked down like a thief caught in the act, as I said to yself, I love you Mercedez, I can't live without you.

About 11 a.m. Mercedez and her brother Tom Mallari returned, knocked at our door and fetched us. Mother and I went to the house of Mr. Santos which was about 3 houses away from our house after the house where Bening, my ex-girlfriend live.

Mr. Santos and family were celebrating for winning the case of their son, Jr. and companions with their lawyer Atty. Santiago.

That's how fast news spread in our village. No wonder when we walked past the house where Bening live, she was watering her plants and looking at us while we passed by their house.

At the house of Mr. Santos I was introduced to the elders' of Mr. Santos, Mr. Mallari and Mr. Taruc. To them I was instant celebrity.

The old folks talked among themselves, "our grandchildren can not file bail because bail was too high, Php30,000 for each of them -- the judge was so strict -- yet our lawyer, discreetly pointing at me with their smallest finger so I will not notice it, had the case dismissed at "first round" like "Elorde when he knocked down Gomes?", first round only.

Mr. Santos even recounted to the elders how strict the judge was, he ordered the Bailiff to "arrest the police-witness for failure to appear "at the hearing.

Mr. Mallari narrated to the elders how the complainant, taxi driver witness could not answer the question of "our lawyer Atty. Santiago "when he asked him:

"Q: why did you not warn the police while they were frisking the passengers that the passengers had a kitchen knife 7 inches long?"

"Taxi driver complainant: Cannot answer".

Then our lawyer Atty. Santiago followed – up his Q uestion with another question:

"Q: Is it because you Mr. Witness knew all the time that the passengers did not have a kitchen knife 7 inches long, because you just made that "Hold-Up Me "story to "frame-up" your passengers the accused in this case?"

"Witness taxi driver complainant: Cannot answer."

At that time all I did was look at Mercedez. My whole being was engrossed looking at the beauty of Mercedez. Her face, her fair complexion skin, so soft and "pinkist", her round black eyes, her kissable lips, her petite body, her legs, her hands, her whole being had mystified me completely, oh la la, she was to me the most beautiful girl in the world, in the universe. For me Mercedez was the personification of every bit of a woman I want to hold and to love forever.

But I am too old for her. She was then only 17 while I was nearly 29 years old.

What will her parents say, what will her neighbors say? While Mercedez may still be playing "tumbang preso or Piko" I was alresady battling with giants of my law profession in the courtrooms of Manila, Quezon City, Pasay, Pasig, Makati, Paranaque, Las Pinas, Malabon, Caloocan, Rizal, Laguna, and Zamboanga, to name a few.

Without my knowing it, but Mercedez confessed it to me later, she had liked me the first time she saw me while she was paraded as one of the princess, "Princesa Engkantada" in the Santa Cruz de Mayo held last year in our village. She was just 16 years old then.

The Santa Cruz de Mayo usually held in one Sunday of the month of May was paraded at the main thoroughfare of the village, causing vehicles, private and public and passenger buses to be stranded for hours. Anyway the long wait was worth the waiting time because of the many beautiful "reynas or queens" and "princesses, of young and beautiful girls about 16, 18 years old" in beautiful dresses and gowns. Mercedez was one of them. I remembered last year, I was stranded while I was driving my "Hillman Hunter Car" along one of the main streets of our village. I looked at a beautiful face, lovely as a rose, far beautiful than "Mona Lisa" or "Venus" or even "Cleopatra" played in the movie by "Elizabeth Taylor" or all of them put together.

As the parade moved on, I thought that will be the last time I will take fancy of her beautiful face. But as time goes by, her face kept on stuck in my mind. I longed to see her again. I want to find her. But I did not even know her name or where she live, how could I find her.

Then one fateful day, Mr. Santos, and his wife and compadres, Mr. Mallari with his daughter Mercedez the kid sister of accused Tom Mallari, and Mr. Taruc came to our house and my Law Office to ask me to fight the case of their accused sons. How delightfully surprised I was when I saw her, the girl of my dreams. I thought to myself, I will ask whose daughter she was. But I could not speak, all I did was to look at her every move and took delight in each smile, in each move she made. Then Mr. Mallari called her, "Mercedez get me my cigarette, to ease my tension" and he motioned to her, and she answered "Yes Papa, I will get your cigarette in a minute", her voice was to my ears so heavenly. Ahha, her name was "Mercedez". I will handle the case of her brother with or without "acceptance fees", so that was how I came to know that Mercedez was the name of the girl of my dreams. My everlasting love. And they want me to be their lawyer for their kin? Of course, with or without "acceptance fees" I will, "Your wish is my command ". All my thoughts and my whole being were focused at Mercedez the girl of my dreams. My magnificent obsession.

After the sumptuous lunch I went out to the backyard of Mr. Santos planted to vegetables as Upo, Kalabasa, Talong, Seguerillas, and other vegetables while savoring the beauty of Mercedez in my mind, and planning how I may tell her "I love you". -- Then, As if in a dream, Mercedez with sweet smile on her approached me with a cup of coffee for me. I thought to myself, "oh what luck, I must be the luckiest guy in this wide, wide world. The girl of my dreams approached me by herself, shall I let her go away? Of course not. I will embrace her and will not let her go. All my thoughts, all my mind, all my being she had engulped me completely. That was it. I forgot everything. All I knew, all I can feel was that I was kissing her lips, her face. I was embracing her and she was embracing me too, so tight I could hear her heart pump strongly and her breath like melody in the air, how long, I could not tell. I forgot the time, I forgot everything. All I knew was that I had the girl I love so much in my arms. All I knew was that I have in my arms the woman I will love forever. There was music in the air, as if a thousand angels were singing "when you are in love... Alleluia... I will not let her go, happen what may.

What will happen next? Bahala na. I must not lose her again.

At the living room of the house of Mr. Santos talk on how the "Vista or hearing" ended in the "Dismissal "of the Case against the accused, their relative and grandchildren went on as lively as one can imagine.

Meanwhile, Mercedez and I were at the backyard then. in tight embrace, in fiery lips to lips.

At the living room the father of Mercedez recounted to the elders how their lawyer, Atty. Santiago mentioned the story of "Juez de Cutchillo" to emphasize the importance of sticking to the "rules on procedural due process", but when the elders began to interpellate him on how exactly the Attorney said his argument, Mr, Mallari urged the elders to ask the "lawyer himself" straight from the "horse mouth" so they rushed to the backyard to ask me, and how surprised they were when they saw us, Mercedez and I in sweet embrace, unmindful of the world..

The elders called my mother and all the elders, as well as the mother of Mercedez, Mr. And Mrs. Santos as host and owner of the house and they all saw us, Mercedez and I still in tight embrace, without caring for the world, then they all coughed loudly which brought us, Mercedez and I to the world of reality. Then the elders asked us to come into the living room to explain ourselves and talk about "our wedding".

The elders had the chairs re-arranged so that we, Mercedez and I sat in the middle and the elders and my mother sat on the chairs encircling us.

"It must be love at first sight. Our 'dalaga' was very young, she was still playing "piko" and "tumbang preso" sighed Aling Nena, mother of Mercedez, but she added, if Mercedez really love Attorney of course I will not object. It is nice to have a lawyer "son-in-law" and she laughed.

My mother commented that she will stand by the side of Mercedez.:

My mother: I like Mercedez. She is so sweet, innocent and beautiful and a respectful child. Whatever decision she will make in this regard, I will sustain her and be with her.

Mang Ato "short for Renato", father of Mr. Gido Mallari, grandfather of Mercedez, said: I am glad to hear the mother of Attorney like our "dalaga"; Let us then ask "the lawyer" as to his intention about our "dalaga".

Atty. Santiago: Grandfather "Mang Ato". Mang Gido, Mr. Mallari, and Aling "Nena", father and mother of Mercedez, Mr. And Mrs. Santos, and all the elders here pressent, I love your "dalaga" Mercedez. I will love her throughout my life, and beyond, I did everything because of my love for her. I am single and I am willing and ready to marry her anytime, anywhere, whenever and whereever she want me to marry her, with your blessings and permission of course.

Mang "Ato": So we have heard the good intentions of the "Lawyer". What do you say, "Mercedez, apo"?, he asked Mercedez.

Mercedez: I love Attorney Santiago, Lolo. Since I saw him last year when I was paraded as one of the "sagala" in the Santa Cruz de Mayo. His car was stranded by the parade, I saw him looking at me and since then I had always thought of him, I had always longed to be with him, anywhere, everywhere. and anytime. I did not know his name, nor his house, but I kept on thinking that someday we will see each other again and then we will never part. So that when he embraced me this afternoon I embraced him too. I would not want to lose him again.

The elders were surprised at the fantastic story they heard. But it happened already so there was nothing to talk about but the day of the wedding.

Mr. Santos and Mr. Taruc commented,: We noticed our "dalaga" and Atty. Santiago exchanged glimpses during the trial of our sons, only we did not give special meaning to it. We even saw Mercedez embraced Attorney when the case was "Ordered Dismissed" by the Judge. They must have "love at first sight".

Mang "Ato": Alright, after what had happened, I want my "Apo, meaning 'granddaughter', Mercedez and Attorney Santiago to be married at once, this coming Sunday at our place, the birthplace of Mercedez at Barrio Dalaga, Magalang, Pampanga.

Mang Gido Mallari, father of Mercedez: Will the Mayor have sufficient time for the documents, Tatang?

Mang "Ato": I will call him at once and I will go back to our province this afternoon to personally follow-up the preparation of the documents for the wedding of my "apo Mercedez and Attorney."

Mr. Lito Santos said: Of course, I will be one of the "Ninong" meaning, sponsor, of the wedding of Mercedez and Atty. Santiago.

At that point Attorney Padolina with a Chinese mestizo looking companion knocked at the half-open door of the house of Mr. Santos as he said:

Atty. Padolina: Good afternoon to all, I am Atty. Padolina. my companion here is Dr. Ching, the son of my long-time friend Frank Tang Bun Ching of Pangasinan. He just arrived from the States. He is here in the Philippines to look after the partition of the estate of his father and get his inheritance so I referred him to Atty. Santiago who is in active practice of the law profession since I am already retired, We went to your house and Law Office, Atty. Santiago but your neighbor told us you were here at the house of Mr. Santos, so we proceeded here.

Atty. Santiago: Thank You, Atty. Padolina, how are you?

Atty. Padolina: I am fine, yet I need complete freedom from worries of court battles, I am not young anymore, so I am referring to you Dr. Ching's legal problems. Atty. Santiago kindly attend to his "inheritance case", Okay? Then he looked at Dr. Ching, and told him: "

Atty. Padolina: Dr. Ching, Atty. Santiago will attend to your legal problems. You are in good hands. Just tell him what you want and it will be done, Okay?

Dr. Ching: Well that's okay with me. Nice meeting you Atty. Santiago and he extended his hand in handshake.

I took his hand and as we shook hands, I introduced Dr. Ching to my mother and Mercedez, as I said:

Atty. Santiago: Dr. Ching, this is my mother, and this is my wife to be, Mercedez. This here is the grandfather of Mercedez, Mang Ato, and this here is her father, Mang Gido, and her mother, Aling Nena, and this here is Mr. Lito Santos and Mr. Nano Taruc, our Ninong or sponsors. You came in the right place at the right time. We were discussing our marriage plans.

Of course, Mang Ato, the grandfather of Mercedez, Mang Gido, and Aling Nena, father and mother of Mercedez, and Mang Lito Santos and Mang Nano Taruc, felt proud and respected being introduced to Dr. Ching, a new client of Atty. Santiago, a doctor from the States, claimant of certain "inheritance".

Dr. Ching replied:

Dr. Ching: This must be the right time to have a new lawyer.

You are about to increase your clan so to us Chinese, that is fortunate day, I will win my case with you Atty. Santiago.

Attorney Padolina then said: Okay so you are all acquainted with one another, I will bid goodbye for now. Atty. Santiago, "bahala ka na" kay Dr. Ching. I will go home and get some rest.

Then Dr. Ching continued, as he sat down near my chair, he said:

Dr. Ching: Actually I have just arrived. Atty. Padolina fetched me from the airport then we proceeded to the VIP Hotel at Dewey Boulevard managed by my friend. and took a room there, I bought his car for my transportation here in the Philippines,.the "Mustang" maroon sedan car parked outside, Then we proceeded here to meet you Atty. Santiago as Atty. Padolina could not attend to my case like he attended to the cases of my father when he was younger. I will go back to the States as soon as we have

111

formalized my case here. So how much will it cost me to file my petition for partition and get my inheritance, Atty. Santiago?

Atty. Santiago: That depends on how much is the estate left by your father, and how much inheritance you want to get from it.

The elders and father and mother of Mercedez were all ears, naturally. Dr. Ching was a stateside client, imagine that?

So I asked Dr. Ching:

Atty. Santiago: When did your father die, Dr. Ching?

Dr. Ching: Last year, 1970 June 24 at the Dagupan General Hospital. I was issued a Death Certificate by his doctor. Here it is, Atty. Santiago. And here is my picture near the remains of my father also in picture. Here also is my "Birth Certificate" to prove my lineage with my father, Franklin Tang Bun Ching;

Atty. Santiago: Where was the last residence of your father, Dr. Ching?

Dr. Ching: Centro, Dagupan, Pangasinan,

Atty. Santiago: How much is the worth of the estate of your father, Dr. Ching.?

Dr. Ching: Php 10 Million Pesos cash in bank; Php 10 Million Pesos real estate properties. Php 5 Million Pesos business "whole sale and retail dry merchandize "; Total of Php 25 Million Pesos.

Mang Ato, the grandfather of Mercedez and her father and mother and Mang Lito and Mang Nano, looked at each other upon hearing the size of inheritance, imagine Php 25 Million Pesos– sangdamukal.

Atty. Santiago: How many creditors did your father have, as you know?

Dr. Ching: None that I know of.

Atty. Santiago: Did your father leave a "Last Will and Testament"?

Dr. Ching: None that I know of;

Atty. Santiago: Besides your mother how many siblings do you, have, Dr. Ching?

Dr. Ching: I have two small brothers, Luis, 4 years old, and Tonio, 6 years old. They live with my mother at Dagupan, Pangasinan.

Atty. Santiago: What's the full name of your father, Dr. Ching?

Dr. Ching: The full name of my father is Franklin Tang Bun Ching, businessman; My mother's name is Luningning San Diego Tang Bun Ching. they were legally married in the Philippines.

Atty. Santiago: What's your full name and citizenship, and your official address in the Philippines. Dr. Ching?

Dr. Ching: My full name is George San Diego Tang Bun Ching, I am a Citizen of the United States of America, having been born in California on May l7 1940. I am a Doctor of Medicine by profession, in California. I have my official address in Rm 234 VIP Hotel, Dewey Boulevard, Manila, Philippines.

In California, USA my official Address is "Nayong Pilipino, 3rd Floor, Rm 345. Manteca, CA-USA.

I want to get the lot located at corner Highway Pangasinan with the Bank of the Philippine Islands on it. Plus Cash of Php 2 Millio Pesos. as my inheritance.

Atty. Santiago: So that will be more or less Php 7 Million Pesos Dr. Ching.

However, under Philippine law, the surviving spouse gets one half of the estate of the deceased spouse as her conjugal share, the remaining half of the estate will then be divided into the number of children plus the surviving spouse having equal share of a child, in your particular case, your mother plus the three children, Luis, Tonio and Dr. Ching will share equally, of the remaining half. That is of the Php 25 Million one half of which Php 12,500,000 Pesos will go to your mother, the remaining Php 12,500,000 Pesos will be divided into 4 equal share, each of you wll be entitled to Php 3,125,000 Pesos.

Dr. Ching: About that much, then how much will you charge me, so you will work it out?

Atty. Santiago: For Attorney's fees, after you get your inheritance, you pay me Cash Php 312,500 Pesos; For Acceptance fees, you pay me Cash Php 70,000 pesos package deal no appearance fees anymore. Filing fees on your account.

Dr. Ching: Okay. Agreed. I will give you now Php 2,000 pesos as downpayment. I will give you the balance of Php 68,000 pesos as your acceptance fees, tomorrow. Do not bother with the receipt now, tomorrow when I have completed my payment you give me the full receipt for acceptance fees.

Atty. Santiago: When was the last time you talked to your mother regarding your "inheritance" Dr. Ching?.

Dr. Ching: Last year, when I learned about my father's death I hurriedly went home. My father was already dead when I arrived. I talked to my mother, Luningning San Diego Tang Bun Ching and asked her to divide the property of my father. She told me that cannot be done because of the clan. That's all, she said..

Atty. Santiago: No reason at all, just that it cannot be because of the clan, Dr. Ching? What about the law?

Dr. Ching: Actually she does not want to partition the estate, although I told her already I personally have seen my father dead at the General Hospital of Dagupan, last year. So partition of the estate and inheritance should follow. Still I could not convince her.

Atty. Santiago: Tomorrow when you come back, we will go to Dagupan and I will talk to your mother, Okay, Dr. Ching?

Dr. Ching: that's okay to me. Tomorrow then. Atty. Santiago: I will wait for you tomorrow morning, Dr. Ching..

After Dr. Ching had left, I turned to Mercedez and told her:

Atty. Santiago: Mercedez let us go to SM Carriedo, at Sta. Cruz Manila so you can buy your gown and shoes and bag and whatever you like for our "Wedding", Let us also buy "Barong Tagalog "with matching pants and leather shoes for your father "Mang Gido", and Ninong Santos and Ninong Taruc, and buy also "Baro at Saya" with Sandals for "Aling Nena", your mother, and "Aling Rosa" wife of Mr. Santos and "Aling

Tindeng" wife of Mr. Taruc for their use at our "Wedding". Here is Two Thousand (Php 2,000) Pesos.

At that time Men's Barong Tagalog with matching pants and leather shoes costs Php 80.00 only so, For Mang Gido, father of Mercedez and Mr Santos and Mr. Taruc a total of Php 240 will be sufficient for three Barong Tagalog with matching pants and leather shoes. Aling Nena's "Baro at Saya" with new "sandals "will cost Php 100.00 only at SM Sta. Cruz, Manila. So, for the three Baro at Saya with matching Sandals, Php 300 Pesos will be sufficient, A total of Php 540 for the Men and Womens' attire. For the gowns and leather shoes for Mercedez about Php 350 will be more than sufficient. I had coat and tie colored "flesh" and leather shoes "crocodile skin" made to order by "Sharp Avenida "costs me only Php 150 Pesos guaranteed finish within 3 days time, ready for pick-up early in the morning, Thursday. My mother had also "Baro at Saya" with Sandals worth Php 100 Pesos.

So at once Mercedez and I with my mother and Aling Nena mother of Mercedez took a taxi so as not to be bothered with driving and parking space; Mang Gido, father of Mercedez and Mang Nano and Aling Tindeng took another taxi, and Mang Lito and Aling Rosa Santos took another taxi, and we ordered the taxi drivers to drop us to SM Carriedo Sta. Cruz, Manila.

For all three taxi fares we paid Php. 55 pesos going to SM. Carriedo, Sta. Cruz, Manila with flag down meters.

After shopping we ate at "Bulakena Reataurant" at Avenida Rizal, Sta. Cruz., Manila. We ate Lechon, Fried Chicken, Menudo, Adobo, Pansit, Mechado, drank 2 cups of coffee, 4 bottles of coke, 3 bottles of beer, for all of which I paid Php 50.00 only. That's life in Manila during those times.

We went home also with three taxi cabs, with flag down meters, and paid Php 54.70 fare only.

The next day early in the morning Dr. Ching riding on his Maroon colored "Mustang "car came to our house and law office and fetched me for Dagupan, Pangasinan. As he promised he handed to me Php 68,000 Pesos the balance of my acceptance fees. I gave him receipt for the full payment of acceptance fee of Php 70,000 for the partition of the estate of his father, Franklin Tang Bun Ching, of Dagupan, Pangasinan.

Before we started for Dagupan, I gave the Php 60,000 to my mother and told her that I took the Php 8,000 Pesos with me for expenses. Then I asked my mother and Mercedez to go with us just like touring Pangasinan to which idea both of them agreed so we went to Dagupan, Dr. Ching, and I and Mercedez and my mother.

At Dagupan, we proceeded to the "Merchandize whole sale retail business of Tang at Centro, Dagupan, Pangasinan at 1st, 2nd and 3rd floor. Dr. Ching pointed to me his "brother Luncio Khu on his mother's side," as the one "impersonating" his father, Franklin Tang Bun Ching, and controlling the merchandize business of the Ching. I asked Dr. Ching to tell me how Luncio Khu became his brother on his mother side, thus:

Atty. Santiago: How did you become the younger brother of Luncio Khu on your mother side, Dr. Ching?.

Dr. Ching: When I went home last year to bade farewell to my father's remains, I saw "Luncio Khu" manning the business of my father so I asked my mother "who was he" my mother told me that "he is Luncio Khu" her son fathered by Fu Khu who kidnapped her from the Philippines in 1936 and brought her to China, and in 1937 she gave birth to Luncio; some years later, she was rescued by my father Frank Tang Bun Ching from Fu Khu and took her to America to evade the wrath of the furious Fu Khu. I, Dr. Ching was born in America. In 1947 my parents came back to the Philippines and were married here. That's all I know about Luncio Khu, ended Dr. Ching..

Then we proceeded to the fourth floor. I told Mercedez to buy "Kodak" and ask for receipt which she did. She was issued a receipt by the 'supposed father' of Dr. Ching who had long been dead. Then we proceeded to the fourth floor, the residence of Dr. Ching's mother, and his siblings.

While entering the business center of Dagupan, Dr. Ching pointed to me the Bank of Philippine Islands on the corner lot of the Provincial Pangasinan Highway and National Highway, which he want as his inheritance plus Two Million (Php 2 Million) Pesos Cash.

Dr. Ching introduced me to his mother at her residence at the fourth floor, while Mercedez and my mother went window shopping at the business establishments around Centro building.

I explained to Dr. Ching's mother that under the law, when a person dies, his heirs has the obligaation to inform the BIR about it for payment of "estate tax" and "inheritance tax" so they have to follow the law and partition the estate. But his mother told us not that she is opposed to it, but that the "clan" will not permit it. Just then, the "brother "of Dr. Ching on his mother's side, Luncio Khu fathered by Fu Khu, joined our conversation and said that no partition of the estate is required while the owner of the estate is alive. So, while Dr. Ching want to have the lot occupied by the Bank of the Philippine Islands and Cash of Two Million Pesos as inheritance, there is no inheritance to talk about as his father is alive.. And he introduced himself as "Frank Tang Bun Ching, and said:

Impostor" Frank Tang Bun Ching: I am Frank Tang Bun Ching.

Dr. George Tang Bun Ching cannot partition the property while his father is alive. As you can see, I am still alive, Attorney.

Atty. Santiago: Mr. Frank Tang Bun Ching, with due respect to what you have just said, my client Dr. George Tang Bun Ching claim that his father, Frank Tang Bun Ching has died last year, he saw his remains, and have secured "Death Certificate as well as pictures of his dead father. Also he had certain credible people willing to testify in his favor. While we do not wish to disturb family relations, but to legally partake of his share in the inheritance, we will be constrained to go to court for the legal partition of the estate.

Mr. Frank Tang Bun Ching: While you may have the right to go to court, Attorney, it will be worthwhile to advise your "young" client that we are all Chinese, although we may have Pilipino Citizenship and your client an American Citizen having been born in California, USA, in 1940 he is still Chinese bound by the code and customs of the clan to which he belongs. The clan has ccertain sanctions we cannot run away from.

Dr. Ching protested, and said:

Dr. George Tang Bun Ching: Our clans' customs and tradition cannot violate laws. Although we respect our customs and traditions we are still bound by the law of the country where we are.

"Impostor" Frank Tang Bun Ching: Ahhh, young blood, always disobedient of old folks.. Attorney, you are far away from Manila where you came from, better go while the sun still shine its light, rumors say there were highway robbers along the highways and dangerous to travel at night.

I sensed a warning and I whispered to my client:

Atty. Santiago: Let's go home and talk about what we will do.

Dr. Ching: Okay.

We bade goodbye to Dr. Ching's mother and went home.

Dr. Ching ask me: Do you drive? Drive my car. Here is the key.

Feel how easy to drive her.

Atty. Santiago: Okay let us go. I will drop Mercedez and my mother at the house of Mr. Santos first so they can continue their talk about our wedding plan, then we will proceed to your hotel, Dr. Ching, Okay?

Dr. Ching: Okay. So, that impostor, the man referring to himself as my father, taking the name of my father "Franklin Tang Bun Ching:" would not want me to have my inheritance. Actually he is Luncio Khu my elder brother on the side of my mother. I saw him at our house last year when I came back to the Philippines to see my father cremated. So he made it appear that "he" was cremated and assumed my father's identity and continued my father's business and bank account. Why my mother was letting him impersonate my father, I could not explain. But surely she has her reason. What shall we do now. Atty. Santiago?

Atty. Santiago: We have to file the "Petition for Partition" and prove that your father has died last year and that your "Father" now was being impersonated by your brother on your mother's side, Luncio Khu.

Dr. Ching: Okay, let us go to my hotel and make necessary preparations.

First, as I am going back to the states tomorrow, I will leave my car, this car for your transportation. I bought this from my friend the Manager of the VIP Hotel for Two Thousand (Php 2,000.00) Pesos only.

Atty. Santiago: It is nice driving it. Since you want to lend it to me for my transportation, maybe it will be better if I give you your Two

Thousand (Php 2,000) Pesos in payment for the car, that way I will have my transportation, and I can insure the car against all risk, own damage and third party liability, so both of us will have no future road problems. What do you say to that?

Dr. Ching: I think that was better I will call my friend the Manager of the VIP Hotel, to prepare the Deed of Sale from him straight to you, Atty. Virgilio J. Santiago and have it's insurance transfered to your name and benefit.

About our case, what will you do now, Atty. Santiago?, Dr. Ching asked me.

Atty. Santiago: I will prepare the necessaary paper for your signature then you can go back to the States. We will just communicate by phone. In about 3 weeks we will have our hearing, maybe by that time you will be back already for our hearing.

Dr. Ching: That will be better. I will go back to the states just to appoint the persons to run my "Day Care and Clinic "in California, and give him the necessary papers to act accordingly.

When we arrived at the VIP Hotel, all pertinent papers regarding the transfer of ownership of the maroon "Mustang Car" from the Manager of the VIP Hotel to my name was already ready for my signature. Mr. Teng, who insured the car against all risks was there too to witness the transfer of insurance, as required.

Mr. Teng: Atty. Santiago, it is nice to know you are handling the case of the partition of the estate of my friend Frank Tang Bun Ching the father of Dr. George Tang Bun Ching. Well, George you are in good hands, Atty. Santiago is a fast worker. You will get your inheritance no doubt about it.

Dr. Ching: I am glad you also know Atty. Santiago, Mr. Teng.

Mr. Teng: I also happen to be one of the clients of Atty. Santiago.

He saved me and my family from an ambitious "hustler".

Dr. Ching: My father died last year, yet some "hustler "has been impersonating him so I cannot get my inheritance.

Mr. Teng: Well you are in good hands,. Atty. Santiago will get it for you.

Dr. Ching: You have the key to the car and the "Deed of Sale" and the Insurance Atty. Santiago?

Atty. Santiago: Okay, it's all with me, you and I will file the Petition for Partition two days from today.

Dr. Ching: Even with my "Impostor Father" alive, Atty. Santiago?

Atty. Santiago: Yes, we will force the issue. So "your father" will be committed to take the position whether to "back off "or 'lie' in court.

Dr. Ching: That will be good, either way, he will lose.

Atty. Santiago: That's the idea. Okay then, I will go now.

So I went back to the house of Mr. Santos in my new 'Mustang Car'.

My mother and the elders, father and mother of Mercedez were still discussing "Mercedez and my Wedding" scheduled for the coming Sunday. at "Barrio Dalaga "Magalang, Pampanga at 7:00 o'clock in the morning.

I greeted everybody with "Good Evening" as it was already 6:00 PM when I entered the house of Mr. Santos, then I greeted Mercedez with a kiss and handed to her Five Thousand (Php 5,000) Pesos and whispered to her, for our "Wedding" preparation, we will buy all we need tomorrow at the Magalang biggest store, like refrigerator, 2 TV sets, 3 electric fans, sofa chairs and marital bed.

That night I prepared the Petition For Partition of the estate of the late Frank Tang Bun Ching, Filipino, of legal age, married to Luningning San Diego Tang Bun Ching, who died at the Dagupan General Hospital on June 24 1970 as evidenced by hereto attached Death Certificate, marked Annex "A"; That his last place of residence for at least six months pror to his death was Centro, Dagupan, Pangasinan; That he left the following as his compulsory heirs: (1) his wife, Luningning San Diego Tang Bun Ching, of legal age, residing at Centro, Dagupan, Pangasinan; (2) Son, George Tang Bun Ching of legal age, an American Citizen by birth, professional doctor., residing at Rm 234 VIP Hotel, Dewey Boulevard, Manila; (3) Sons Luis Tang Bun Ching, minor, 4 years old, under the care of his mother, Luningning San Diego, Tang Bun Ching; and (4)

Tonio Tang Bun Ching, minor, 6 years old under the care of his mother, Luningning San Diego Tang Bun Ching;; (5) That he left no debts nor creditors; (6) That he left the following real and personal properties: (6-1) One lot 1,500 square meters at corner Dagupan Provincial Highway and National Highway covered by TCT No. 2345678 in the name of Franklin Tang Bun Ching, Filipino, of legal age, married to Luningning San Diego Tang Bun Ching, of legal age, Filipino with address at Centro, Dagupan, Pangasinan. (6-2) Lot 1,500 square meters, with building 4 storey known as "Centro Building, covered by TCT No. 3215678 at center of Poblacion, Dagupan, Pangasinan; With goods and merchandize known as "Centro Dry Merchan- dize "In the 1ˢᵗ, 2ⁿᵈ and 3ʳᵈ floors;

Wherefor, it is respectfully prayed of this Honorable Court of Dagupan Pangasinan that the estate of my late father, Franklin Tang Bun Ching be partitioned among the heirs aforementioned in accordance with law.

Manila for Dagupan, Pangasinan.
June 20 1971.
George Tang Bun Ching y San Diego

Petitioner
Rm 234 VIP Hotel, Dewey Blvd, Manila
Assisted by: Atty. Virgilio J. Santiago
56 Lanzones Street, Proect 2, Quirino District, Quezon City;
Tel. 209 – 957-0670
Vjsan51536@yahoo.com

The next day, I went to VIP Hotel and had the Petition For Partition signed by the Petitioner, Dr. George Tang Bun Ching y San Diego

After which we, Dr. Ching and I went straight to Dagupan, Pangasinan and filed the Petition.

Atty. Santiago: We have done the first step, Dr. Ching. We will just wait for the action of the court.

Dr. Ching: Okay, I will prepare to go home to America tomorrow.

Just call me of any development, Atty. Santiago..

Atty. Santiago: I will do that. For now, I will attend to our "wedding plan" with Mercedez.

So after dropping Dr. Ching at his hotel, I hurried to go home to attend to our "Wedding Plan" with Mercedez..

As it was already Friday and our wedding was scheduled for Sunday, I asked Mercedez to go shopping at the department store at Magalang, Pampanga where we bought 2 TV sets. One for the sala, and the other for the bedroom. Refrigerators, one for the kitchen, another for our room, sala set and sofa and marital bed, 3 electric fans and had them delivered to the house of Mang Guido and Aling Nena Mallari whom they know of course as they have been province mate for a long time, and Mercedez the daughter of Mang Guido was with me. All of the said furnitures and appliances cost us Php 5,500 Pesos only. Then we, Mercedez and I pro- ceeded to the "Best Cooking Lechon Store" and ordered 2 lechon de Leche 2 feet long each, and 2 big lechon 4 feet long each, to be delivered to the house of Mang Guido and Aling Nena on Sunday at 11 a.m. for all of which lechon cost us Php 2,500 Pesos only, which we paid half of its price Php 1,250 Pesos and the balance to be paid on delivery. I told the owner his store was recommended by the Mayor, so make it "extra crispy and good tasting."

Then we went to the "Best Carinderia" known for tasty cooked food and ordered Menudo, Mechado Adobo, Fried Chicken, Pansit and Lumpiang Shanghai good for 200 people to be delivered Sunday morning about 11 a.m. and paid half of its price as downpayment and the balance on delivery to the house of Mang Guido and Aling Nena Mallari at Barrio Dalaga, Magalang, Pampanga, which of course they know well as they have been province mate for such a long time and also because I have with me my wife to be, Mercedez whom they have known from childhood. Total of the cooked food we bought cost us Php 1, 750 only. That was how cheap food was then.

When we returned to the house, the 2 TV sets, one for the living

room and one for our room of Mercedez, Sala Set, sofa, refrigerators, one for the kitchen and another for our room of Mercedez, 3 electric fans, marital bed, with cushion, were already delivered. Tom Mallari and the other relatives of Mercedez were all at hand and set the furnitures at the designated part of the house as per instruction of Mercedez. Mercedez looked very happy, she must be like playing "bahay-bahayan" and ordered her "kuya Tom "and other relatives left and right who followed her without objection as they knew Mercedez was the star of the occassion then and will be married to a "somebody", a lawyer.

Of course when sleeping time came, Mercedez and I tried to sleep on the marital bed. But it seems that all ears were on every move we make so that we had not slept at all.

I thought that everyday consisted of 24 hours, but I felt that the longest day was Saturday, and took all my patience waiting for Sunday, for the day of "our marriage, Mercedez and my marriage".

Very early the next day, Sunday, I had my bath and got ready for the happy occassion, our "marriage, Mercedez and mine". I put on my new Coat and Tie from "The Sharp "and my "Crocodile Skin shoes "Mercedez was already all set with her new "Wedding Gown" and "Leather high hill Shoes" Then at 6:45 AM our abay, Ninongs and Ninangs, my mother and the parents of Mercedez and the elders and Mercedez and I, all happily troop to the house of the Mayor who is the grandchild of Mang Ato, the grandfather of Mercedez on the father's side. The Mayor officiated the marriage ceremony. After the ceremony, at the "formal declaration" of being "husband and wife" the Mayor jokingly gave the "Marriage Certificate "to Mercedez and told her, "Chedeng, here is your "Marriage Certificate", don"t lose that, otherwise "Attorney" might say he is "single "and you have no proof anymore. So everybody laughed.

Mang Ato invited the Mayor and his officials and their wives and children, to the house of Mang Guido for lunch.

Then we went back to the house of Mang Guido, where my "Mustang Maroon Sedan Car" was parked. That time, "Mustang Car" was a rarity.

The Mayor looked around to see where the Mallari was cooking the food we will eat at lunch time but saw that people sat at the chairs and benches talking about the wedding and the "stars of the wedding" but no one was cooking food anywhere.

At the house of the Mallari the Mayor and his officials Mang Guido and Aling Nena and Ninong Taruc and Santos and their wives, my mother, Mercedez and I, sat at the new Sala set, some sat at the sofa, and others on the benches, and watch TV at the Sala. The Mayor joked, this sala set and TV must have just arrived yesterday, they were still "hot". Other visitors sat on the chairs and benches at the balcony and still other visitors sat on benches at the backyard and around the house, It was as if "fiesta ng bayan." While we expected about 50 persons, about 200 persons came to our wedding celebration.

Everybody seemed to wonder where the food for lunch is. Then the restaurants where we ordered the 2 Lechon de Leche 2 feet long each and 2 big lechon 4 feet long each came. Aha, there were lechon, which looked crispy and still hot. Mercedez's mother, Aling Nena ordered the lechon to be brought to the kitchen where she ordered them chopped properly.

Next came the restaurant where Mercedez and I ordered the Menudo, Mechado, Adobo, Lumpiang Shanghai, Pansit, and Fried Chicken good for 200 people came. Aling Nena, the mother of Mercedez again took charge as to where in the kitchen will they be brought for preparation for lunch.

At lunch time, all were satisfied. The food was delicious and abundant and other visitors were even able to "take home" some food. It was like "fiesta ng bayan", a whole day affair. Even their relatives and elders who live from the outer parts of the Barrio came to our wedding when they heard that "Mercedez will marry" the lawyer who saved their 'kin and/or grandchildren from the "balulang" meaning "jail". Mercedez and I were very happy. So was my mother who looked at me and said, "You see son, if you were not a lawyer, you will not be able to touch even the hand of your wife Mercedez, a very beautiful young girl. I smiled in full agreement.

I smiled once more and looked up and said, Thank you Lord God Almighty, Praise be Your Name Forever. You made everything possible.

Chapter XI

Chinese Do Not Die
In the Philippines

(Names*fictional/events factual)

After a month, I received throsugh the Manager of the VIP Hotel an Answer with prayer to dismiss the Petition for Partition of the Estate of the Late Franklin Tang Bun Ching filed by Petitioner George Tang Bun Ching y San Diego on the legal ground that Franklin Tang Bun Ching is still alive and therefore no estate was left by him, no reason at all to partition the estate. A Resolution of the Court was also received by the Hotel Manager which "Dismissed" the Petition on the ground alleged in the Answer of respondent Franklin Tang Bun Ching.

I scrutinized the "Answer" of respondent. It was signed by Franklin

Tang Bun Ching, who according to Dr. Ching was a fake. being impersonated by Luncio Fu khu, his older brother on his mother's side.

Which if true as may be proven by evidence, Luncio khu will go to prison for "Falsification".

I immediately called Dr. Ching by long distance and told him the Petition For Partition of the Estate of his father Franklin Tang Bun Chin was "Dismissed "by the Court of Dagupan Pangasinan, as we have expected, on the basis of the "allegation of the Answer of Franklin Tang Bun Ching himself" that "he is still alive.".

Dr. George Tang Bun Ching then asked me.:

Dr. Ching: What shall we do, Atty. Santiago?

Atty. Santiago: The answer committed your "impostor father" to " "run "or to "lie" in court, I replied. If he run, then you will get your "inheritance"; If he "lie" in court, then he gets imprisoned for "falsification" and you get your "inheritance". Either way you get your "inheritance".

Dr. Ching: Okay, I will come back to the Philippines, as soon as possible. I will call you then, Atty. Santiago.

Atty. Santiago: I will wait for you.

Sometime later, I received several telephone calls asking for an appointment regarding the case of Dr. Tang Bun Ching, "to talk about the Case so no one will lose explaining to me that in court battle there is always a winner and a loser, however, in talking about the matter of the case everybody wins, to which I agreed, so we set an appointment for a meeting in neutral grounds.

A meeting was set at Aristocrat, Dewey Boulevard at sunset 6:00 o'clock Monday. The voice said I do not know him but she knew me. So that must be a puzzle. Anyway, I told the voice, I am interested.

Come Monday in brown "coat and tie" at exactly six pm I was already sitting at one of the tables of Aristocrat at Dewey Boulevard facing the setting sun, with a cup of coffee.

Then from behind me the voice identical with the voice I talked to the telephone said:

The Voice: I am glad you came. Atty. Santiago.

Atty. Santiago: I said I would come to our meeting so I did. I am also glad you came. When I turned my head at my back I was surprised to see a beautiful woman standing behind me. But her voice was that of a man. She was a gay.

Atty. Santiago: "Kindly sit down".

The Voice: I see you do not discriminate. I am a man-woman. My name is Lita, little woman, little man. Lita. How are you Sir.

Atty. Santiago: I am fine Thank you Lita. I wish we wil have a mutual benefit with this meeting, and I smiled.

Lita: I also wish that it will be.

Atty. Santiago: Well, Lita, what's your interest in this case of Dr. Ching?

Lita: Personally I will be affected by this case, she confided. You see, I am one of the siblings of Franklin Tang Bun Ching, the "impostor"..I came here from China when I heard about this case of Dr. Ching.

Atty. Santiago: Oh, is that so? Why are you telling me this Lita?, I asked her or him.

Lita: Well as you see, Atty. Santiago, I can be a he or a she, depends on my options. In China, the code and customs of the clan are highly respected. Any disrespect of the code or custom may result to banishment, temporarily or forever, or even death depending on the "decision" of the elders of the clan. There are three major clans: The Khu, the Ming and the Tang. My brother, Luncio Khu, born in China 1936, the one on the shoes of the father of Dr. Ching now, belongs to the Khu clan. His father being Fu Khu, also my father, but different mother. Our father Fu Khu snatched Luningning Sandiego in 1936 from the Philippines and brought her to China. She was then 15 years old, very beautiful, one year after, she gave birth to my brother Luncio Khu, born 1937. My father hurt his wife, Lumcio's mother, whenever he gets jealous so Franklin Tang Bun Ching, the father of Dr. Ching took pity of her and snatched her at an opportune time in 1937 after she had given birth to Luncio Khu. Franklin took Luningning away from Fu Khu and brought her to America. Fu Khu swore he would regain her and kill Franklin any minute he found him. I was born in 1939 by my mother Lynlin, an abandoned child of the "Ming" Clan working as helper in the Khu clan. After I was born, my father Fu Khu abandoned my mother and me to look for Franklin and Luningning in the Philippines, and kill them both to avenge his "man's ego" but he was killed in 1943 in the Philippines by the Japanese during the Japanese-American war. All of these were written in the Khu Clan Book. The Ming clan then took care of me and my mother.

In 1949, Luncio was then 13 years old, he slipped in the Philippines and managed to survive in the streets and learned the illegal trades. He was a member of "Triad" a brotherhood of gangsters known for "Murder for hire," "Robbery", "Kidnapping" "Illegal Drugs" and other unthinkable "unlawul activities" in China with alliance in the Philippines. His mother, Luningning knew all these so that to appease her son by Fu Khu, she cooperated with Luncio Khu. Luningning gave birth to George Tang Bun Ching in California, USA in 1940 while she and her husband Franklin Tang Bun Ching were hiding in America from the wrath of Fu Khu known as a violent, unreasonable man. In America good fortune blessed Luningning and Franklin Tang Bun Ching. They prospered and became rich so that when they returned to the Philippines in 1946 and brought their dollars with them they had greater advantage over other chinese merchants and became extra prosperous in the Philippines. When Franklin Tang Bun Ching died in 1970, my brother Luncio Khu took over the business concern of Franklin Tang Bun Ching as he impersonated him with the cooperation of his mother Luningning, whom he threatened to "massacre his siblings, George. Luis and Tonio, on his mother's side."

Atty. Santiago: What about you Lita, how are you affected by the case of Dr. George Tang Bun Ching?, I asked.

Lita, answered: While I do not have direct involvement in the case of Luncio Khu, if per evidence Dr, Ching can show that "Chinese do not die in the Philippines" as in the case of my brother Luncio Khu, who made the remains of Franklin Tang Bun Ching cremated as Luncio Khu then assumed the name of Franklin Tang Bun Ching and continued the business concern of the Tang Family, with the support of the influential Khu family and with the cooperation of his mother Luningning so as to appease her son Luncio and make him desist from executing his threat of harming George, Luis and Tonio his siblings in his mother's side.

To estabilize the situation, the elders of our "Clan" may come to a decision to "remove" the cause of the disturbance of the peaceful continuity of the "social, commercial. and political condition and 'order' the male members of our clan to execute the "order" at all cost. As you see, Atty. Santiago, behind my image as a woman, I am a "male member" of our clan. That's how I am affected.

Lita took a deep breath, then contined:

Lita: I requested this meeting so that you and I might find possible reason to prevent any unfortunate outcome of the case of Dr. Ching, your client may bring about,. Atty. Santiago.

Atty. Santiago: I see your point Lita and I appreciate your heavenly concern.

I thought to myself, George, Luis and Tonio are all blood -relations of the "Tang Family", so it is possible that the elders of the Tang will not just "watch silently" as the saying goes, "Blood is thicker than water". Then there will be blood bath.

So I told my opinion, to Lita:

Atty. Santiago: I think the better way to deal with this situation is for the "Khu clan" to 'order Luncio' to desist from his 'threat' of harming his siblings on his mother's side, George, Luis, and Tonio, how, I do not know. My client Dr. Ching may be persuaded not to 'insist' on his claim for 'inheritance' if his share will be respected by giving him its equivalent in Philippine pesos, if that is possible, and the 'Khu" clan Elders will be amenable, what say you Lita?

Lita: I will try to see other options that may be open, I will call you again, and thank you Atty. Santiago.

Then Lita smiled at me just like a woman "flirting".

I thought to myself, Lita may like me because I treated her with respect and without discrimination as to his being a gay. That will be helpful to our case of Dr. Ching.

Dr. Ching came back to the Philippines and dropped by my office as soon as possible. I greeted him pleasantly and told him about the meeting I had with Lita. Dr. Ching was surprised. I showed him my tape recorder and let him hear my conversation with Lita.

Dr. Ching: Then I am in dangerous situation, also my mother and other small brothers at Dagupan, Pangasinan, he commented.

Atty. Santiago: That seems to be the case, Dr. Ching. So what do you want to do now?. I asked Dr. Ching.

Of course I do not want to push him. Let him decide for himself. I will do as my client instruct me as long as it is legally possible, but I should not be "more popous than the pope", as the saying goes.

Dr. Ching: What do you think, is the best move Atty. Santiago?

He threw the ball back to me.

Atty. Santiago: Well depends on your determination to get your inheritance although there is a risk or danger, we can consider on putting pressure on your "impostor father".

Dr. Ching: Like what, Atty. Santiago?

Atty. Santiago: Like getting the "Impostor arrested" by the NBI for "Kidnapping" or "Coercion" and filing "Case of Undesireable Alien "for him to be deported.

About his threat of "eliminating" your minor siblings, we will ask the opinion of the NBI on whether it is an "immediate" threat or last option on the part of the "Impostor". As to your personal safety, of course we can ask for "bodyguard" don't you think so, Dr. Ching?

Dr. Ching: So we file case of "Undesireable Alien", where? Of course not at Dagupan Pangasinan, he must have some "influence "there, Atty. Santiago.

Atty. Santiago: Not at Dagupan, Pangasinan, Of Course.

Dr. Ching: So, where?, Atty. Santiago?

Atty. Santiago: At the Congress of the Philippines. Your "Impostor Father "is an "Undesireable Alien" he should be removed from the Philippine soil. He should be "deported" at once.

Dr. Ching: Right, that's correct.

Atty. Santiago: Now, Dr. Ching, this signature on top of the typewritten name Franklin Tang Bun Ching, Respondent on the "Answer" of your "father" to the "Petition For Partition", is this the signature of your father?,

Dr. Ching: If I had not seen my father dead at the General Hospital of Dagupan Pangasinan, I will say this signature was geneuine.

Atty. Santiago: We will force a hearing of our Petition to declare your brother "John Doe "as an "undesireable alien" for (1) "impersonating Franklin Tang Bun Ching", your father and (2) taking over the business concern of the Tang Family and (3) committing "Grand Scale Estafa", by (4) issuing "Checks" in the name of Franklin Tang Bun Ching, destroying the faith of the public in Commercial papers, "impersonating your father Franklin Tang Bun Ching, (5) using the BIR ID impersonating Franklin Tang Bun Ching transacting business with the BIR defrauding the Government, all of which acts amount to "Undesireable Alien".

So as planned, I immediately filed the following petition:

"Petition To Declare John Doe an 'Undesireable Alien'"

I, Dr. George Tang Bun Ching y Sandiego, of legal age, a Citizen of the United Sates of America, residing at Rm 234 VIP Hotel, Dewey Boulevard, Manila, after being duly sworn according to law, hereby deposes and say:

1. I am the son of my father Franklin Tang Bun Ching and my mother Luningning Sandiego, married to each other, both Filipino citizens, with residence at Centro Building, Dagupan, Pangasinan;

2. That I was born in 1940 in California, USA, hence I am a Citizen of the United States of America.

3. That my father, Franklin Tang Bun Ching died in Dagupan General Hospital, Dagupan, Pangasinan, on June 24, 1970, as evidenced by hereto attached Death Certificate issued by the attending Physician, Dr. Simon Torre a resident Doctor-Physician of the Dagupan General Hospital, marked Annex "A";.

4. That Pictures of myself with my dead father in the stretcher, showing his face were taken by the official photographer of the Dagupan General Hospital, at my request.;

5. That under the law, the death of a person has to be reported within certain number of days not more than one (1) year to the Bureau of Internal Revenue and within 2 days by the Hospital and/or attending Doctor/Physician to the local civil registrar.

6. That sometime June 20 1971, I filed with the Court of First Instance of Dagupan, Pangasinan, a Petition For Partition of the Estate of my Father, Franklin Tang Bun Ching, alleging among others, as follow:

Petition For Partition Of The Estate of The
Late Franklin Tang Bun Ching-

I, Dr. George Tang Bun Ching, of legal age, USA Citizen, residing at Rm 234 VIP Hotel, VIP Buiding, Dewey Boulevard, Manila, a Doctor of Medicine by profession in California, USA respectfully alleges:

1. That my father, Franklin Tang Bun Ching died on June 24 1970 at Dagupan General Hospital, Dagupan, Pangasinan, as evidebced by Death Certificate hereto attached, marked Annex "A" issued by the attending Physician Dr. Simon Torre;

2. That my father's last residence was Centro Building, Dagupan, Pangasinan;

3. That my father left no "will" or "last testament:;

4. That my father left "no creditors" known to me;

5. That my father left the following "real and personal assets" as follows:

Real Properties: 1 lot 1.500 square meters located and situated at corner National Highway and Provincial Highway of Pangasinan with Building of 4 storey floors, covered by TCT No. 3456789 of the Registrar of Deeds of Dagupan, Pangasinan; Worth Php 10 Million Pesos; 1 Lot 1,500 square meters located and situated at Centro Dagupan, Pangasinan, with Centro Building on it with 4 storey floors, the 1st, 2nd and 3rd floors are devoted to Merchandize Store; and the 4th floor devoted for residence of the Tang Family; covered by TCT No. 4321900 of the Registrar of Deeds of Dagupan, Pangasinan; Worth Php 10 Million Pesos; Personal and movable properties/Merchandize on the 1st, 2nd and 3rd floors of the Centro Building, worth Php 5 Million Pesos;

6. That my father left the following compulsory heirs named as follows:

    a) Luningning Sandiego Tang Bun Ching hiswife, Residing at 4th floor Centro Building

b) George Sandiego Tang Bun Ching, of legal age, Doctor of Medicine, US Citizen, Son, residing at Rm 234 VIP Hotel, VIP Building, Dewey Boulevard, Manila;

c) Luis Sandiego Tang Bun Ching, Minor, Son, under the care of his mother, Luningning Sandiego Tang Bun Ching, residing at 4th Floor, Centro Building, Dagupan, Pangasinan;

d) Tonio Sandiego Tang Bun Ching, minor Son, under the care of his mother, Luningning Sandiego Tang Bun Ching. Residing at 4th Floor, Centro Building, Dagupan, Pangasinan.

7. That a "John Doe" person claiming to be my father Franklin Tang Bun Ching had filed an "Answer "to the "Petition For Partition" opposing the partition on the ground that "Franklin Tang Bun Ching" is alive and therefore his "Estate" canot be partitioned by and among the mentioned "compulsory heirs";

8. That the "John Doe" person claiming to be my father Franklin Tang Bun Ching is an "Impostor" impersonating my dead father;

9. That I am ready and able and I have such evidence, as "Death Certificate" and "Pictures "of my dead father, Franklin Tang Bun Ching and other testimonies of persons who knew my father Franklin Tang Bun Ching and can attest to the fact of his death and can likewise prove that the "John Doe" claming to be my father Frabklin Tang Bun Ching is an:Impostor, and an "Undesireable Alien" and violating the laws of Immigration, the Bureau of Internal Revenue and the basic policy of the Republic of the Philippines and should be "Ordered deported Immediately" after service of the sanctions of the law.

Wherefore, premises consiered it is respectfully prayed that a hearing on this Petition be "Ordered" and the "John Doe" be "Ordered placed in the "Legis Custodia" of the Honorable Senate of the Republic of the Philippines,' until a full investigation of the "Senate Blue Ribbon Committee "is finally terminated.

Respectfully,
George Tang Bun Ching y Sandiego- Petitioner
July 27, 1971, Rm 234 VIP Hotel, VIP Building,
Dewey Boulevard, Manila

Assisted by: Atty. Virgilio J. Santiago 56 Lanzones Street,
Project 2, Quirino District, Quezon City; Tel. 209-957-0670
Sponsored by: Hon. Hedyboy Hilarde *, Senator
July 27, 1971, Manila

News on the "Petition To Declare an "Undesireable Alien", the John Doe impersonating the deceased Franklin Tang Bun Ching who died June 24 1970 gave rise to a daily news question "Is it true that Chinese do not die in the Philippines?

Other newspaper daily proffer the question: 'True or False ""Chinese do not die in the Philippines?

Other people muse "Chinese die but were reincarnated by their relatives who assume their names, status and "Immigration papers" through the cooperation of "corrupt" immigration officials.

After a week or so, Lita called me by phone, and said:

Lita: Atty. Santiago, this is Lita, we must meet again at the same time and place, tomorrow, Okay?.

Atty. Santiago: Okay, Lita, see you then.

The next day, at exactly 6:00 o'clock in the evening, I was at the Aristocrat at Dewey Boulevard at the same table I took then with a cup of coffee.

I was viewing the setting sun when newspaper men and TV program Newscasters like DzAB and DzBZ surrounded me and bombarded me with questions, like:

Question: "Atty. Santiago, is your client Dr. Ching determined to put in "Jail the 'John Doe' impostor?"

Question:"Atty. Santiago, how much will make your Client Dr. Ching suffer "amnesia"?

"Atty. Santiago, how much will it take for your Client to "fly back to the States? "

To all such questions I just answered:

Atty. Santiago: Any and all answer I give here will be "hearsay" and "inadmisible" in court proceedings, so I better say "no comment", my friends.

Some media men were so persistent that I had to answer, thus:

Atty. Santiago:"My client will appear in Congress, then you can ask him personally, Okay, my friends?:

Some TV newscaster question me "Who are you waiting here,   at Aristocrat, Atty. Santiago, Sir?

Atty. Santiago: I am waiting for some feelers who might want to know what I feel may happen in Congress, and I smiled.

After some time, the media men and ladies disappeared. Then I heard the voice of Lita.:

Lita: Thank you Atty. Santiago for coming to our meeting. How are you now?

Atty. Santiago: I am fine, thank you, and how are you, Lita?

Lita: The elders were discussing the probable outcome of the case of your client, Dr. Ching, Atty. Santiago. Especially the latest "Petition to Declare the "John Doe Impostor" an "undesireable alien" Dr. Ching filed with Congress.

Some Elders said there are other clans apprehensive that some of them being similarly situated may be directly affected and so disturb their social, business and political condition in the Philippines.

Some say even those in abroad may be indirectly affected and placed in doubtful situation and so hamper their progress. All these will be more serious If Congress will continue to termination their investigation and end with appropriate impasse law to the "impostor".

Atty. Santiago: So what's in their mind, Lita, have they made any decision yet?

Lita: So the elders have thought of a "recall", no more aid to the "Impostor" and worst "to bring him back to China by 'force' "by the 'male members' on condition that no "real property or "immovable" shall be 'dissipated' as per agreement of the parties otherwise the elders will "recall" the impostor" but will move into the situation and impose its will.

Atty. Santiago: In the last situation "inheritance" and even the family of Tang will all be banished and erased, is that what it means, Lita?

Lita: Exactly. I think the better option is situation no. 2, that is "recall" of the "impostor by force" on condition that the parties "agree" that no "immovable" shall be dissipated, then the "Elders" will sanction the "inheritance agreement", that is the 'better of the worst.'

Atty. Santiago: Okay, Lita, thank you and please call me again to let you know what my client will say. The Senate had scheduled the "hearing "of the Petition by the Blue Ribbon Committe at 2 PM next Tuesday, I will call a meeting with my client tomorrow then please call me a day after tomorrow, Lita. I gave Lita a goodbye kiss on the cheek.

After Lita had left, I immediately drove my "Mustang Car" to VIP Hotel a few blocks away from Aristocrat.

Dr. Ching: What happened with your meeting with Lita Atty. Santiago?

I always make it a point to inform my client Dr. Ching of whateve r meeting I will have with any party connected to his case to remove any doubt.

Atty. Santiago: Here is my tape recorder, hear yourself what happened with our conversation, Dr. Ching.

Dr. Ching: So, what do you say we should do, Atty. Santiago.

Atty. Santiago: We have to decide and tell the "Elders our decision before the "Senate hearing". According to you, you want to have the Lot at corner Provincial Highway and National Highway, which you value at Php 5 Million plus Php 2 Million Cash, total of which is Php 7 Million as your "Inheritance"; According to the law, One half of the total Estate or Php 12,500,000 is "conjugal property and belongs to your mother; The other half of the estate Php 12,500,000 belongs to the heirs to be divided equally among themselves meaning Php 12,500,000 pesos divided by 4 heirs, Luningning, Dr. Ching and Luis and Tonio, equals Php 3,125,000 pesos Cash for each heir, but the condition of the "Elders "was no "immovables" shall be dissipated or lost or sold; Your mother Luningning do not want to sell the lot, your minor siblings, Luis and Tonio being minors had no say as to "sell or not" the "immovables", As to your "Inheritance", of Php 3,125,000 there is sufficient Cash in Bank so if you are amenable to receive your "inheritance in Cash" then there is no more "problem" the "Impostor" will be "recalled" to China and will no longer be in a position to "harm" any of his siblings.

Dr. Ching: After receiving my "Inheritance in Cash" I can go back to America and attend to my "Day Care Clinic" and can come back to the Philippines every now and then as I please, with no more problem.

What about our case in Dagupan, Pangasinan, Atty. Santiago?

Atty. Santiago: No problem about that. It was "Dismissed: and will stay "dismissed" until You move to "re-open for reconsideration.". Which I suppose would better be in "status quo".

Dr. Ching: What about the Senate Case? I was summoned to appear at the "Hearing of the Blue Ribbon" scheduled for next week.

Atty. Santiago: I will attend the Senate Hearing as your counsel.

Dr. Ching.

Dr. Ching: Alright then, I am already amenable to receive my "Inheritance in Cash Php 3,125,000 Pesos. I will give you 10% of that minus Php 70,000 so I will still give you Php 242,500 Pesos. Okay, just give me Php 2,882,500 Pesos. When will I get my "Inheritance"? who will give me the Cash, Atty. Santiago,? asked Dr. Ching..

Atty. Santiago: Actually I do not know from where the Cash will come from; or as to who will give it to me for you and what receipt I will prepare for it; But I will tell you immediately once I receive it. You see I will be at risk doing this just to finish the case, this is somewhat an extraordinary under the table deal although Not Illegal, it is also not so legal but as long as it satisfy my client and all parties to the agreement, I think nobody will complain about it, and when there is "No complainant, there is no case".

Dr. Ching: As soon as I get my money, I will fly back to America. I have my plane ticket already, you will accompany me to the airport to answer any "inquiry", from the Press, Okay Atty. Santiago?

Atty. Santiago: Okay, Dr. Ching

At the lobby of the VIP Hotel I was surrounded by the media people and questioned, thus:

Press Media: Atty. Santiago what did your client Dr. Ching say, will he appear at the Senate Blue Ribbon Commitee?

Another group of Press People ask: Will Dr. Ching do a "Houdini"?

Atty. Santiago: Please my friends, I cannot answer your questions. I was not told as to what my client "will do" and I cannot "prophesied" nor preempt what "he will do". Anyway any answer I give will be "hearsay" and "inadmissible" being "mere opinion."

The Press even made a "count down" of the days to the Senate Blue Ribbon Hearing.

Then while questions by the Press and the Media were hurled at me as the "Senate Hearing "of the "Issue of ""Chinese Do Not Die in The Philippines" was hot as "Hot Cake" and was considered "of general public concern," Lita called me by phone and asked for an "Immediate" person to person meeting at "Tagaytay Vista Lodge with a room already reserved, prepared and paid for me "at 2 PM the next day.

The next day, I drove to Tagaytay Vista Lodge and at exactly 2 PM

I inquired at the "Information" about the room already reerved, prepared and paid for a "lawyer" without giving my name. I was ushered into a big nice room where there was a chair and a table with a cup of hot coffee on it in the middle of the room, and seven (7) elegant chairs facing it. I was surprised by the arrangement of the chairs so I attempted to leave the room but Lita appeared and told me that the preparation was that way because the elders, some seven of them will appear and state their mind. Then it will be for me to respond but Lita told me that will be the first and the last meeting with the Elders and with her/him. The outcome of the meeting will be of my decision. But the final say will be for the Elders. Lita is with the Elders, so he told me, being considered as among the "male" enforcers - members of their clan. I readily sensed that my decision will determine whether I will come out of the room in good health or I will not be seen again as a case of a "disappearance" ala "Houdini style".

So I told myself, "Bahala na". I will do as my best discretion and intuition tell me.

Then in a minute or so, the seven "Elders of the Clan" entered in their customary clothing Chinese "silk" attire, very colorful. They all looked respecttable, rich and authoritative.

Although I was in my best "coat and tie" I think they were not "impressed "as my attire for them must be "ordinary and casual" only.

Anyway, the spokesman of the "Seven Elders" said:

Spokesman: We admire your courage, Atty. Santiago. Courage imply sincerity. We appreciate also your coming meaning that you agree with the intention of our clan for peaceful outcome of the case of Dr. Ching, your client. For our purposes we do not consider beneficial any dissipation of the "immovable" portions of the "Inheritance" of Dr. Ching. But we can compromise with his intention by giving him Cash sufficient to buy his peace, and protect his mother and siblings by "Order" of "recall" of the "violent impostor".

Then the spokeman looked me over from head to foot and from foot to head.

I of course felt "insulted" but I smiled and I said:

Atty Santiago: Respectable one, I am sorry if my attire was not so pleasant as this is my "uniform" in attending to my profession; yet I found honored of facing the "Elders" of the clan which I will treasure in my memory in my old age.

Of course I could not say how I managed to say those expressions but I felt the "Elders" were pleased with my humble sincerity.

Then the spokesman, continued:

Spokesman: Well said, young man. To continue, we offer Php 4,500, 000 Pesos to buy peace. Once accepted by the "young man Atty. Santiago", it will be a "done deal", Dr. Ching will leave the Philippines and all cases will be lost in dream and forgotten forever. Senate Investiga- tion will be abandoned. The young man representative-lawyer of Dr. Ching will personally see the "Deal Done" as stated here. The mother and siblings of Dr. Ching will be fully protected by the Clan.

The spokesman then told Lita:

Spokesman: Lita bring in the "offer".

Lita brought out the "Golden Suitcase" and told me to see its contents and count them if I want.

So I opened the suite case and found Php 4,500,000 Pesos in Php. 1,000 Peso bills.

I took the suitcase and said "Thank you Lita".

Lita: You made a wise decision Attorney. Goodbye.

I stood up and took the suitcase with me and hurried to my car.

I felt like many eyes were trailing me as I walked to my car and drove back to our house.

At home I called up Dr. Ching and told him to prepare to fly back to America. I took out all the money bills from the Golden Suitcase and trans- ferred it to my old suitcase. Then I took out Php 2,882,500 Pesos and placed it in a paper bag and placed it inside the golden suitcase. I then hid my old suitcase among my old clothes.

I then bade my mother goodbye and told her I will take Dr. Ching to the airport.

When I arrived at the VIP Hotel Dr. Ching was already ready to go to the airport to fly back to America. I gave him the paper bag with the Php 2,882,500 Pesos. I explained to him that the Clan will protect his mother and Luis and Tonio Tang Bun Ching y Sandiego. His "impostor father" had already "been recalled" to China by the "Male" members of the "Clan", so there is no more threat to think about his safety. All cases both in Pangasinan and Senate Petition abandoned. That's the deal.

Dr. Ching agreed to all the terms of the deal, and said:

Dr. Ching: I agree to all their terms. Thank you Atty. Santiago. I will deposit my money at the airport and give your money at the airport.

Atty. Santiago: Dr. Ching, That's alright. I have separated my money from yours already. I thought I will not get out of that place anymore. When I walked out of our rendezvous I felt I had been paid already. Anytime the

"Elders" can "order" their "male members" to have me eliminated, forever. So we better stick to our side of the agreement, Okay, Dr. Ching?

Dr. Ching: Okay, Atty. Santiago.

On the way home, I stopped a minute along the Dewey Boulevard and threw away the "golden suitcase" into the bay.

Then I looked up and made my fervent prayer as I said:

Atty. Santiago: Thank You Lord God Almighty. Praise be Your Name Forever. Amen.

At home I called Atty. Padolina,:

Atty. Santiago: Good Evening, Atty. Padolina I called just to tell you your "sobre "is here ready for the taking. Kindly pick it up.

Atty. Padolina: I will pick it up now.

I gave the "sobre" with Ten Thousand (Php 10,000) Pesos to my mother to give to Atty. Padolina when he picked it up.

Then I drove to Barrio Dalaga, Magalang Pampanga and fetched my wife Mercedez. We checked in at the Manila Hotel and enjoyed our "First Night" without any interference.

At the hearing of the Senate Blue Ribbon Committee, Dr. Ching was absent.

I was present but when Media people asked me about the whereabout of my client, Dr. Ching, my answer was simple:

Atty. Santiago: I have no personal knowedge of Dr. Ching's where-about, Your Honors,. Anyway, whatever place I say he is now, will be incompetent and hearsay and inadmissible as second hand information.

The Senators just laughed.

Another Senator said: The Case for hearing was not yet open, so there's nothing to close.

Other Senators were heard to say: "No complainant, No Case". "So there's no case to close.

I looked up once more and prayed:

Atty. Santiago: I Thank You Lord God Almighty. Praise be your Name Forever. Amen.

********** Copyright (c) 2010 by author, Virgilio J. Santiago **********

Chapter XII
A Case Of Violation Of Hippocratic Oath

(Names* fictional/events true and factual)

One night during the Martial Law declared by then President Marcos, while curfew hour was being strictly enforced between 11 pm and 5 am of the following morning, I was rushing my wife Mercedez, now known as Carmencita or Carmen or Nene to the Fabella Maternity Hospital in Sampaloc, Manila, for profuse bleeding, as she was having a miscarriage of our 6 month old baby. We were walking slowly though huriedly when we were stopped by Metrocom soldiers manning a police outpost enforcing curfew hour.

A soldier in full battle uniform asked us:

Soldier: Where are you going?

I politely answered:

Atty. Santiago: I am Atty. Santiago, I am rushing my wife to Fabella Maternity Hospital. She was having a miscarriage of our 6 month old baby.

The soldiers saw my wife bleeding so they took pity on us.

Soldier: Hop in our Metrocar, we will bring you to Fabella Maternity Hospital.

Upon reaching the Fabella Maternity Hospital I hurriedly asked for the assistance of people attending the Information service. I told them my wife was having a miscariage of our 6 month old baby and need medical assistance at once. But nobody seem to pay attention to me so I asked for the doctor on duty, A doctor with ID name Mangulat approached us so I told him my wife was having a miscarriage of our 6 month old baby and need urgent medical assistance but that doctor, Dr. Mangulat refused to admit my wife-patient as according to him my wife's condition was apparently an illegal abortion case and the hospital do not admit such kind of emergency cases so as duty doctor then, he will not admit my wife-patient. That made me furious, so I told him in a loud voice:

Atty Santiago: Doctor Mangulat, that's your name, is it not?, Okay doctor, let me tell you this, you do not want to admit my wife-patient because as you said, my wife's condition was apparently a case of illegal abortion and Fabella Hospital do not admit such cases -- Doctor Mangulat, your reason for not admitting my wife is unacceptable to me as it was a mere conclusion of fact without basis in fact and in law. As you have said "Apparent"' case of illegal abortion -- You or any doctor in this hospital, the Fabella Hospital has not made as yet any examination of my wife's condition and you have already made a declared reason for not admitting" my wife-patient? Let me remind you Doctor this Fabella Maternity Hospital is Government-run hospital -- meaning your salary and all the salary of doctors, nurses and everybody here, janitors and guards included, are being paid by taxes we the people are paying the Government -- you are only our employees -- you do not have any righ to refuse us -- Understand.?

Dr. Mangulat having realized the truth of my statement, could not speak.

So I continued:

Atty. Santiago: Alright, Dr. Mangulat, I am giving you a warning -- If morning comes and still you do not attend to my wife-patient, I will go directly to the Fiscal's office of Manila and file criminal charges against you -- for refusing to admit a patient, for coercion, for unjust vexation, for negligence and ignorance of law resulting to injury and emotional distress, I will go also to the Professional Regulatory Commission and have your license revoked and cancelled for not attending to patient in emergency case.

Because of the noise I was making then, the director of the hospital went out of her office and asked me:

Director: I am the director of this hospital, what seem to be the problem?

Atty Santiago: I am Atty. Santiago, madam Director, I have here my wife-patient, as you can see, my wife is bleeding, she was having a miscarriage of our 6 month old baby -- however, your doctor here, Dr. Mangulat says his ID, is that his correct name, madam? I asked her – so the Director nodded – to continue, Madam Director, your doctor on duty here, Dr. Mangulat, refused to admit my wife-patient as he told me my wife's condition was an apparent case of illegal abortion -- Your doctor on duty had not yet examined the patient yet he had already made a conclusion of fact, so I had given him a warning I told him "if you will still refuse to admit my wife-patient, as soon as the sun shine in the east, I will go straight to the Fiscal's office of Manila and file criminal cases against you for coercion, unjust vexation, reckless imprudence, refusal to admit a patient in emergency case, -- and I am also warning you Madam Director, if you shall refuse also to admit my wife-patient then I. will also file criminal charges against you which will be more serious than what I will file against him as you hold a higher position.

"I will also file against you Madam director and against Doctor Mangulat violation of "Hippocratic Oath", a pledge embodying a set of code of ethics, taken by those about to receive a degree in medicine requiring them to treat all persons without consideration of age, sex, race, color, creed, religion, nationality, citizenship, military attachment, civil affiliation, social standing, friend or foe which may result in cancellation of your license to practice medicine here and elsewhere.

Now, Madam Director, let me remind you that the first and primary duty and obligation of any doctor and this hospital for that matter is to treat people in emergency situation, my wife needs medical assistance, I will ask you again, and I said it very loudly "are you admitting my wife-patient or not?"

Madam Director: Yes Attorney Santiago, we will admit your wife and I promise you we will give her proper medical assistance and attention. We are sorry for the inhospitable attitude my people has shown you..

Then the Director turned to her staff and ordered: "Admit the patient.. move. "bilis... bilis.."

I looked up as I murmured: "Thank You Lord God Almighty, Praise be Your Name forever, " Amen.

This episode was included to emphasize that when in the right, fight it out for "No One is above the Law".

Chapter XIII

A Case Of Child Abuse

(Names*fictional/events factual)

One day, I had just been to my court hearing and was relaxing when my granddaughter Maria came home, her hair disheveled, with sour face, and sobbing, so I asked her:

Atty. Satiago: Maria, why are you crying? I asked her.

Maria was then a Grade V pupil of a government-run elementary school, about 10 years old, the daughter of my son Expo.

Maria answered, still sobbing:

Maria: My teacher Ms. Juliet de Leon did this to me. I was sitting on my chair in our classroom. She went out. My classmates played and fooled with each other, and quarreled while our teacher, Ms. De Leon was out of the room. When our teacher, Ms. De Leon, came back and saw the desk and chairs disarrayed, she got angry and asked us, who caused it. My classmates pointed to me to escape liability. Ms De Leon approached me and asked me who caused it. I answered her "I do not know Mom." Then I just kept quiet. She asked me of other questions. I did not answer anymore. I just kept quiet. She got angry at me and scolded me then she held me by my hair, while saying "when I ask you Maria, you answer ha? Ha?, "and pushed my face flat on my desk which caused the bruises on my face, also my head ache. My hair got entangled and disheveled. I got so

---

embarrassed. Then she told me to bring my father to school tomorrow for my misbehavior. I do not want to go to school anymore, Grandpa.

Atty. Santiago: It's okay Maria. Don't worry, I will talk to her. Meantime, you eat your lunch.

Maria: I do not want to eat Grandpa. I lost my appetite.

Atty. Santiago: Okay then, we will go to the public hospital, first for medical treatment and medical certificate of your bruises on your face, and your headache, then to the photo studio to have your bruises and physical condition photogtaphed, then to the police station to report and complain of the physical and psychological abuse you suffered from the hands of your teacher's brutality, and then to your school to talk to your teacher and the principal of the school.

After we had gone to the public hospital for Maria's treatment of her bruises and her headache caused by her teacher Ms. Juliet De Leon and had secured "medical certificate" of her injuries, we went to the photo studio and had pictures of Maria's personal condition and bruises picture taken, then we went to the police station to file our our complaint against her teacher Ms. Juliet De Leon and secure copy of police blotter.

Afterwards we then went to the Principal's office of her elementary school, the principal greeted us:

Principal: Good Afternoon, I see Maria you have brought your father to school—

Atty. Santiago: Good Afternoon, Mr. Principal. I am Atty. Santiago, the Grandfather of Maria. I came to inquire what happened to Maria. She came home this afternoon crying, her hair disheveled, her face with bruises, and with headache. When I asked Maria what happened to her she said her teacher Ms. Juliet de Leon did it to her. She said she does not want to go to school anymore. she was upset. May I talk to her teacher, Mr. Principal.

Mr. Principal: Oh, the bruises on Maria's face do not look serious.

Atty. Santiago: Mr. Principal, Ms. Juliet de Leon being one of your teachers in this school, is under your supervision and control that was why we came to you so you may investigate why Maria suffered bruises on her face, and why her head ache, why Maria had disarrayed hair, why Maria would not want to go to school anymore. I was not asking you Mr. Principal whether the bruises on the face of Maria was serious or not.

Taken- a-back by my curt statement, the principal said—

Mr. Principal: Alright, Ms. Sexta, please call Ms. De Leon and tell her Maria and Atty, Santiago are here regarding her reported incident of Maria's misbehavior this morning.

The remark of the Principal "regarding the reported incident of Maria's misbehavior" pricked me. To think that Ms. De Leon had already condemned my grandchild Maria as "having misbehaved" so that she, Ms. De Leon had reason to lay hand on her. An afterthought alibi.

After a while Ms. De Leon, the teacher of Marria came and said:

Ms. De Leon: Good Afternoon, I see Maria brought her father to school already. That's better so that her misbehavior may be properly assessed by her elders.

Atty. Santiago: Good Afternoon to you Ms. De Leon, I am Atty, Santiago, Maria is my grandchild, the daughter of my son, I was dismayed when Maria came home this afternoon crying, her hair was disheveled and her face with bruises, and her head ache, as you can see, so I asked her what happened to her. She narrated that while she was in your classroom, you went out and while you were out, her classmates played and fooled around. Some quarreled with each other and caused the disarray of the desk and the chairs. When you came back, you got furious and asked your pupils what happened, nobody answered, then you asked who caused the disorder in the room, and you picked Maria to tell you who caused the disorder of the room. Maria said she did not know who caused the disorder of the room. Then you asked some more questions which Maria did not answer and so you got angry at her and scolded her, and embarrassed her in front of her clssmates. On top of that, you maltreated Maria by holding her hair and pushed her face flat on the top of her desk causing her bruises on her face, and caused her head ache. Now Maria would not want to go to school anymore. She was psychologically and physically brutalized by you, Ms. De Leon. What can you say about that, Ms. De Leon.

Ms. De Leon: Atty. Santiago, when the classmates of Maria pointed her to me when I asked "who caused the disorder in the room", I asked Maria - Who caused the disorder of the room.?" "She answered me" "I do not know Mom", So I asked her again, tell me who made the room disarrayed - Maria did not answer me.

And even though how many times I questioned her, she did not answer anymore so I got furious and had touched her hair.

Atty. Santiago: And you caused bruises on her face, and headache and scolded her in front of her schoolmates without reason which caused her so much embarrassment, and untold emotional distress, then you told Maria to bring her father to school for her "misbehavior". You even reported the incident to your Principal as an incident of Maria's misbehavior -- Ms. Juliet de Leon, don't you think you owe Maria an apology – she may be young but you unreasonably castigated her, and maltreated her unlawfully and unjustly. What can you say to that?

Ms. De Leon: Why should I apologize to her, she is just my pupil.

I have the right to discipline my pupils.

Atty. Santiago: Well you may have the right to discipline your pupil, but discipline your pupil in accordance with law. You have no right whatsoever to lay hand on your pupil. That was why we have laws, to abide by the law. There is what we term, "Dura Lex Sed Lex" the law may be harsh but it is the law. We have Republic Act 7610 known as the law for the protection of children against child abuse. Mere shouting, threatening of children, causing them to suffer psychological and physical injuries, causing them emotional distress are instances of violation of this law.

What can you say now, Ms. De Leon.

Ms. De Leon: I still won't apologize to Maria. I have the right to discipline my pupils.

Mr. Principal: That's correct Atty. Santiago. Ms. De Leon has the right to discipline her pupils. We have the right to discipline our pupils, otherwise our pupils will not obey us anymore.

Atty. Santiago: I would not argue with you, Madam De Leon and Mr. Principal, but since there is the law on protection of children against child abuse we have to follow the law, as no one is above the law and since you Mr. Principal are abetting Ms. De Leon 's unlawful conduct in violating the law on protection of children against child abuse, and after having given you Ms. De Leon fair chance to apologize to Maria, yet you still maintain your adamant gesture and wrong belief of disciplining your pupil as reason to violate the law on "child abuse" we bid you "adieu" and we will proceed now to the proper authorities to impose upon you the sanctions of the law which you violated.

The following day I filed the Complaint of "Maria Santiago, child-abuse victim versus Juliet de Leon, her teacher, and the Principal of the Elementary School, Mr. Tiburcio Miron, both as Principals in Violation of the Law on Protection of Children Against Child Abuse" with the Prosecutor's Office of Quezon City..

After due hearing and investigation the "Information" or formal charge of the Violation of the Law on Protection of Children Against Child Abuse entitled "Maria Santiago, child victim of child abuse versus Juliet De Leon, teacher, and Principal Tiburcio Miron, accused, with recommended bail of Php 4000 Pesos for each accused was filed by the Prosecutor of Quezon City with the Regional Trial Court of Quezon City.

Both accused Juliet De Leon and Tiburcio Miron filed bailbond with the Court for temporary liberty pending hearing of their case.

I looked up and thank God Almighty and once more said:

Atty. Santiago: "Thank You Good Lord, God Almighty, Praise be Your Name forever." Amen.

In the following days after this incident, newspapers printed factual stories on child abuse resulting to death of children in grade schools. No doubt such news items will produce favorable influence towards conviction of accused in child abuse cases, hence Ms. Juliet de Leon apologized to Maria in her class to appease her and make her withdraw her case.

As usual and as her nature, Maria just kept quiet.

The hearing, which has always been postponed at the instance of the "defense" is still going on, as of this writing.

Chapter XIV
A Man Deserves Another Chance

(Name*fictional/events true and factual)

My wife was saved from her profuse bleeding due to miscarriage of our 6 month old baby and while recuperating, one of the hospital's nurses approached me and requested me:

Nurse: "Atty. Santiago will you please help my provincemate, Anita", her father has been in jail for a long time already, we do not know what to do," as she called Anita and motioned her to come to us.

A young maiden brown in color, petite and charming looking approached us at once upon the "nurse" biding, and said:

Anita: Good afternoon, Atty. Santiago. I am Anita, my friend and province mate told me you can help us, so I came -- will you help my father, he had been in jail for a long time already, his case has always been postponed, what shall we do?". She asked me.

Atty. Santiago: What's his case,?, I asked Anita.

Anita: My father was charged of illegal recruitment with estafa for "bouncing Checks", he could not put up bail so he was in jail while his case was always postponed. I tried to bail him out, but the bailbond agent asked me Php 24,000 pesos for all his cases, I do not have that much money I have only Php 12,000 pesos.

Atty. Santiago: How many cases have your father, and what were these cases?, I asked Anita.

Anita: Atty. Santiago, 20 cases Illegal Recruitment with Bouncing Checks (Eestafa) with recommended bail of Php 3,000 Pesos each pending with Metropolitan Trial Court of Quezon City, Branch 39 and 20 cases of Illegal Recruitment with Bouncing Checks (Estafa) with recommended bail of Php 3,000 Pesos each, pending with Metropolitan Trial Court of Quezon City Branch 38. I want my father to be bailed out, so he may work to pay his complainants.

Atty. Santiago: The Bailbond Insurance Company is actually apprehensive giving your father bail as if he will jump bail, the insurance company will pay Php 120,000 Pesos; Still I will try if we can bail out your father with your Php 12,000 Pesos only. The insurance will surely ask for collateral of house and lot with Title, you know, I told Anita.

Anita: That's true, the insurance company did asked me to give collateral of Title, Anita agreed. But it is better if we can bail my father out so he can earn money and pay the bouncing checks.. I and my friend nurse will attend to your wife while you are out, Atty. Santiago--; I will give you now the Twelve Thousand (Php 12,000) Pesos for the bailbond of my father, just in case you convince the insurance company to give my father bailbond. Thank you Atty. Santiago.

So that afternoon I went to VIP Building at Dewey Boulevard to see Mr. Teng, the President and Owner of an insurance company issuing bailbonds. I found Mr. Teng at the VIP Coffee Shop relaxing so I approached him and greeted him,:

Atty Santiago: Good Afternoon, Sir. May I sit with your table?

Mr. Teng: Of Course, you are my lawyer, I was impressed with the way you handled the defense of the laundry woman. She is now working for my wife at home. How are you now?, Mr.Teng asked me.

Atty. Santiago: I brought my wife to the hospital yesterday, she is now fine and recuperating well, Thanks to God, -- in the hospital I was requested by the nurse attending to my wife to help her province mate whose father is in jail pending hearing of his cases of Bouncing Checks, in the City Court of Quezon City. She want to bail him out.

Mr. Teng: How many bailbonds is needed to bail him out, how much is the worth of each bond? Mr. Teng, asked me.

Atty. Santiago: 20 cases of "Illegal Recruitment with bouncing Checks with Php 3,000 Pesos bail recommended for each case filed with Branch 38 of the City Court of Quezon City; and 20 cases of "Illegal Recruitment with Bouncing Checks" with Php 3,000 pesos bail recommended for each case, filed with Branch 39 of the City Court of Quezon City., Sir; I answered.

Mr. Teng: Are you handling his defense, Atty. Santiago?

Atty. Santiago: Yes, Sir. I want him out so he can work and pay his bouncing checks, so the complainant will withdraw their complaints, without complainants, then the Illegal Recruitment cases will also be dismissed.. I answered Mr. Teng.

Mr. Teng: So, I will issue the bailbonds. You are his guarantor, okay?

Atty. Santiago: Okay, and thank you. Sir.

Anita almost jumped with joy when I told her her father was issued the 40 bailbonds required for his temporary liberty, so he can work and pay the complainants in the bouncing checks -- I told her that I was the guarantor of her father, and that his father must always appear in court whenever he is so ordered by the court.

The father of Anita, Sergio Maclat as per the bailbonds issued by the Insurance company, was released from confinement pending the hearing of his cases conditioned that he will appear in every hearing of his case when so ordered by the court.

After sometime, the father of Anita, with some help of his other children, was able to pay all the complainants in the bouncing checks, so they agreed to dismiss all cases both the Illegal Recruitment and the Bouncing Checks cases.

I looked up and once again uttered: "Thank you Lord God.Almighty, Praise be Thy Name forever." Amen.

********** Copyright (c) 2010 by author, Virgilio J. Santiago **********

vjsan51536@yahoo.com

Epilogue

Actually there is no end to this book, as court trial extraordinay experience in the Philippines or elsewhere will continue to be experienced by any lawyer, be he of "ordinary" or "extraordinary "caliber as long as he believes in "No one is above the law" and "Nothing is impossible with God", so much so that he focus all his effort, preparation and attention to the defense or attack of the case he is handling "to attain truth and justice as a tribute to glorify and honor God Almighty ", "The Omnipotent One ""The Omniscient One ", "The Creator of All". "The Supreme Judge of All ".

Remember Companeros y Companeras, in the Philippines and elsewhere, the law profession give us not only treasure, pleasure and honor, but most of all, it gives us the right to right a wrong. So, in closing, please let me say: "See you in court".

Virgilio J. Santiago, author
Philippine Lawyer

--End--

Copyright(c)2010 by author, Virgilio J. Santiago. All rights reserved.

Except as permitted under the Copyright Act of 1976, no part of this book may be reproduced in any form or by any electronic or mechanical means. including the use of information storage and material systems, without permission in writing from the copyright owner. Requests for permission should be addressed in writing to

Virgilio J. Santiago at 2610 Presidente Street, Stockton, CA-95210
USA; vjsan51536@yahoo.com

Tel. (209) 957-0670

----------------000----------------

Watch for the coming book II

The Revenge of "Kumintang"
Peace Be With You
The Face Off Solution
The "Resbak"
Quid Pro Quo

www.ingramcontent.com/pod-product-compliance
Lightning Source LLC
Chambersburg PA
CBHW032017170526
45157CB00002B/738